All Goes on Twenty

Second Edition

James Canada

BALBOA
PRESS
A DIVISION OF HAY HOUSE

Balboa Press books may be ordered through booksellers or by contacting:

Balboa Press
A Division of Hay House
1663 Liberty Drive
Bloomington, IN 47403
www.balboapress.com
1-(877) 407-4847

ISBN: 978-1-4525-5807-3 (sc)
ISBN: 978-1-4525-5808-0 (e)

Printed in the United States of America

Balboa Press rev. date: 08/29/2012

Contents

About the Author

James Eugene Canada, (nickname, Jeep), was born in the Blue Ridge Mountains of Virginia on September 30, 1932. The author lost his mother when he was six years old and was raised in the Presbyterian Orphan Home. He spent 10 years of his life there.

Canada joined the Marines at age 17 and spent 20 years in the Corps, retiring in 1969. He fought in two wars and was wounded three times, once during the Korean War and twice during the Vietnam War.

His duties in the Marines were as a drill instructor, Pathfinder in First Force Recon Company and gunnery sergeant in K-3-1. While an instructor on NBC Warfare, he taught most weapons and tactics courses and guerrilla warfare school. He attended jump school at Fort Benning, Georgia and earned his jump wings.

Canada received his A.A. degree at Mira Costa College and attended Pepperdine for two years. His hobbies are gardening, fishing, stamp collecting, writing, and poetry. Many of his poems have been published. This is his third book to be published.

His last book, "We Few, We Chosin Few," received a five-star rating from Amazon. The California Legislature gave him a Certificate of Recognition in Honor of Literary Excellence on March 23, 2005.

Canada was a member of the Chosin Few and attends the reunion of his Korean War outfit each year. He also participates in a local high school's yearly event wherein the veterans tell the students about their experiences and the students put on a show for the veterans.

Acknowledgements

This story began in 1939. Because I have received so many emails with questions about my previous books, I had to start all over again to make the whole story understood. Even now, I receive emails from people who lost a loved one in the two wars in which I fought. I do not get as many emails as I used to regarding the Korean War. The majority of questions are about the Vietnam War, even though it ended more than 40 years ago. There are still sons, grandsons, nephews, daughters and other family members who want to know about their loved ones from that war.

I personally want to thank Dorothy Kalaveras, "artist at large," for her help in putting this book together. We went to Dorothy in 2000 looking for a sign for our reunion. H-3-5 used the sign that she made for quite a few of our reunions.

Dorothy did all the drawings for my last two books, "War Emblems" and "We Few, We Chosin Few."

She also did the drawings and sketches for this book. She has done outstanding work in the city of Oceanside and surrounding area.

Last but not the least is my wife Eliz, who put up with all the questions and spell checks that I bugged her.

Chapter One

The Orphanage

There is always something before then and something after now. Then started on December 7, 1949, when I joined the Marine Corps. I was 17 years old and brought up in an orphanage home. My sister, brother, and I were sent there by the state of Virginia in 1939. I spent 10 years of my life there and grew up strong.

Looking back on the day I left the orphanage on December 6, I will always remember it being cold. Also, it was close to Christmas and hard saying goodbye to all my friends. Breaking the bond after all those years was not easy. That day I left one institution for another.

The Marine Corps had given me bus fare to downtown Lynchburg, a bus ticket to Richmond, Virginia, and a meal ticket for breakfast the next morning. The thought of not making the physical had entered my mind—and where I would go if they turned me down. I could not go back to the home.

It was almost a mile from the orphanage to the bus stop. There was a full moon out, and it was not only cold, it was crisp cold and so still. My ankle was still sore from the sprain I suffered at our last football game. This was the reason I worried about taking the physical.

I remember the day we entered the home. It was after Christmas, and all the toys we received on Christmas had to be left behind. My brother Billy was eight years old, I was seven, and our sister Janie was six.

Every kid had to work no matter how young he or she was. At seven, I was given the job of going to the woods and filling two bags with leaves for bedding for the cows. When there was snow on the ground, you not only had to find the leaves, but they could not be wet. If those two bags were not tightly packed, you would be sent back to fill them all the way up. It did not even matter if it had gotten dark.

The kids who went in the home in 1939 and 1940 are in the following picture. My brother is the fourth boy from the left. I am the fifth boy from the right. Our sister is the fourth girl from the right. I do not know who the grownups are.

Picture 1 – Kids from Home in 1939-1940

As a kid got older, he would be given a new assignment. It could be milking the cows at 4:30 in the morning, feeding the pigs, or, during the summer, working on the farm. There was a job that had to be done at the heating plant also, and our cottage was heated by steam. Being woken up in the morning with the radiator clanging and banging was a normal routine during the winter.

The girls' job was to take care of the kitchen, fold the laundry, wash the pots and pans, and set the tables for mealtime. During the summer, they helped with the picking and canning of strawberries. When these events happened, the boys enjoyed it, because they got to work together.

Dating was out in the early years; the dining room had the girls on one side and the boys on the other. Later when I was about to leave, it became a little more liberal, and the boys began dating the girls. There were quite a few marriages. It is funny, but I cannot remember any divorces.

When I was still in the small boys' cottage, I remember a wedding taking place between Gordon Bragg and Margaret Wirth. It was just before WW II started.

I was one of those kids always in trouble. They had a system for everything, and you could get a whipping, restriction, loss of allowance or a black mark for which you would have to work on the only half day off, Saturday.

One time when I (along with a half a dozen other boys) was on restriction, the kids all went to see the Lynchburg Cardinals baseball team play. After they left, we broke into the canning area below the gymnasium and ground up 20 bushels of apples, pressing out the juice and filling up cans we used for canning.

We forgot to clean up the mess, and it did not take long before they followed the smell to where we hid the cider. The smell was so strong I do not know why I thought we could get away with it.

Christmas was always fun at the home. Soon mail trucks were arriving, and we all got close to see what names we could make out. We opened our presents on Christmas Eve, and there was always a brown bag full of goodies.

My sister and I had not spent a Christmas together since 1948, and when she came to my home in 2009, I surprised her with that brown bag. I remember there was hard Christmas candy, nuts, raisins and fruits. She cried when I gave it to her.

One time during the summer while bringing in the hay crop, I rebelled. I think I was between 14 and 15 but still in the small boys' cottage. Four of us who were close friends did this crime together. We knew we would get a whipping, but we went anyway. When we came through the barbed wire, one kid said, "I pity you, they are going to bust your tail." I said, "Not me, I'm not going back." Burke and Hubert sided with me, but Joe chickened out and went back. We spent the night in the hayloft and collected eggs in the morning, boiled them on a stump that had been burning for a couple of days in the woods. We also poached some horse corn just as the southern boys did in the "War between the States." It is like popcorn but only half popped.

The only money we had was 50 cents that Burke had hidden under his mattress. We waited until everyone went to breakfast, and then got the money. It is funny that I still remember what we bought with it: a pound of bologna, a loaf of bread and a nickel box of matches. By the time it took them to catch us, 11 more boys had joined our gang.

It was September, and anyone who knows Virginia weather knows it was starting to get cold. We had 2 blankets and 13 boys, not enough cover for all the boys. We held out 14 days before they caught us. The three of us who started this adventure had to ride back while the rest walked. They gave the ones who were gone the longest the most punishment.

Now as I bent over the table to take my whipping, I could see all the boys peeking in the window. If I cried, I would lose my rep as being a hard guy. If I did not cry, they would beat harder. Of course, my pride was at stake, so I gave it my best shot.

Picture 2 – Orphanage

The orphanage sat on a hill. The red clay of Virginia was the base for good farming, and, as you can see in the picture, the buildings are in almost half circle. Going from right to left, the big boys' cottage is first and then the teachers' cottage; number two small boys' cottage, number three small boys' cottage, administration building, small girls' cottage, and large girls' cottage. Later they added another building.

In the administration building, there was a storage room and the dining room, office space with two classrooms, a kitchen and stockroom on the first floor. The second floor had the chapel and two more classrooms. The basement had a coal cellar, a can and jar storage room. There was a porch coming off the kitchen and a wood cutting room at the end of the building. There was a cold room where we stored the dairy products and made the butter and cheese. Next to this was the printing room. In the photo, you can see the swimming pool. I was the first one in the year of 1948, when it was only half-full of water.

Below was the heating plant with a laundry and ironing room. There was a smoke house where we hung the hams and a potato storage shack. Almost all of this was gone when I went back in 2003. The gym was turned into the chapel, and the old chapel area was turned into office space.

I remember that the laundry had the coal storage that caught on fire several times during my time there. In addition, this was where all the boys got their haircut. Mr. Mayberry used hand clippers that seemed to pull out half your hair. This was also, where I made candy on a forge.

One day I had made candy and wrapped it in paper to take to school. The candy was so hard that one could not break it. I had a pocketknife, and I tried to stick it, but the knife bounced off and went into my leg. It was just before the bell rang to start class. Blood was spurting out, and I fell to the floor.

We had been trained in first aid in the Boy Scouts and one of my friends added pressure to the area to stop the bleeding. All the girls were standing over me, and the only good thing to come out of this was seeing all the colors of their panties. Then I was rushed to the hospital.

Three things that I loved at the home were playing football, my pet pig Oinkey and my Red Rider BB gun. Every time I see the movie, "The Christmas Story," I remember what a thrill that gun was. The home started up in 1920, and they had a football team that became famous. Ripley's Believe It or Not wrote the article in 1941. Enclosed is that article. Just before World War II, we had another great team. As the war started, they all went off to war.

Picture 3 – Football Team at the Home

My age group did not have anyone to coach us, so we did not have a team until after the war. Gordon Bragg came back; then Earl Blackburn took over. We Shoeless Wonders played barefooted in the snow. The psychological impact on the opposing team was unbelievable. More of our age group left, and in my last year at the home, we only had 12 kids. Docky Ayers was the water boy until someone got hurt. This means that you had to play the whole game. The team that came later was good and had better football equipment.

All the kids were white when I was growing up, and it was only after I left that they took in other kids. Back during the Vietnam War, they started taking kids from there. Now most of the kids who go to the home do not stay long. They do not work on the farm. All the milk cows are gone along with all the farm equipment.

I attended the reunion in 2003 and was so heartbroken to see all the woods sold off and all the memories that I grew up with gone with the wind. I have not been back since then. No kids, that I knew, had come back. The last word was that the home might go bankrupt.

Something seems to be a big secret. When I arrived at the home, the superintendent was Dr. Meggenson. He left soon, and Dr. Moore took over. He was there most of my 10 years, and Dr. Bain took over two years before I left. In all the history written about the home, there is not one word that Dr. Moore was ever there. He did many good things, like sunset services on the front lawn, watermelon and ice cream parties, and canning veggies from the crops grown on the farm.

For kids like me who had nowhere to go on vacation, we had a great time at a place called Goshen Pass. Something happened that erased all that time from history. It is almost like our history books being changed to look better.

Of the many kids who passed through the orphanage over the history of the home, there are many who turned out great. You will find different professionals like doctors, lawyers, judges and teachers.

Some kids also disappeared from the face of the earth. My brother Billy had two friends, the Hicks brothers, who were always together. They used to hide in the closet and draw cartoons and laugh for hours. Billy went back for years looking for them, but he died never having seen either one again.

The Presbyterian Church had a system wherein someone would send Christmas presents to each child. I only remember this happening when I was 15. I lucked out by getting the ladies of Bethesda, Maryland In 1948 they asked me what I wanted for Christmas, and I said a radio, I received an old radio, which I really loved. Up until then the only means of communication was a crystal set that John Witt would let me listen to sometimes. What a thrill to hear the Grand Old Opera.

I do not think there was a boy who did not spend some time cracking nuts during the fall. We had black walnuts, hickory nuts and hazelnuts. When it was a little cold, the best place was in the sun by the gym. In addition, apples were to be had if one knew where to get them. We learned to be survivors.

In all the time at the home, we had only three deaths. I do not know any details on the first death, but I remember the last two: Lloyd Ayer and Daniel Moore drowned in the James River. My brother almost went under also. Dan had a sister, and Lloyd was the first kid who befriended me when I arrived at the home, He picked me up and carried me around on his back. He had three brothers.

We also had our share of diseases. One boy got polio, one girl contacted scarlet fever, and I got typhoid fever. The only good thing to come out of this was that when we were quarantined we got to run wild in the woods instead of going to church and school. Then there were those usual childhood diseases like chicken pox.

Some kids came and stayed until they finished school, and some were taken back by their parents or adopted. Some came back to the reunion each year, and some never came back. There were those who had good memories and those who hated the place.

I was one who remembered both good and bad, but it made me the man that I am today. In fact, I truly believe that if it had not been for the things that made me hard, I would have never survived the Chosin Reservoir.

During the war in 1940, we had a lot of snow and sleet. There were two things that one needed: roller skates and a sled were those things of joy. Living on top of a hill made skating and sledding great fun. The big drawback was pushing the milk cart up the hill. Sometimes we had to hook up the horses to get the milk to the kitchen area. All those memories and then some passed through my mind as I left the home.

Chapter Two

Recruit and Drill Instructor

The Mississippi River is the dividing line where east of the river all recruits go to Parris Island and west they go to San Diego. I went to Parris Island as a recruit. Years later, I was a drill instructor in San Diego. Parris Island was a great area for training, whereas San Diego had too many distractions. They were testing aircraft, and the San Diego Airport had aircraft taking off and landing all the time. If that was not enough, the recruit could see downtown, and those lights at night were too much for some of them.

I went to Parris Island in 1949 and graduated in March 1950. While I was there, I met a recruit named Joe Catts. Joe was a boy from Chicago who came from a middle class Catholic family. He had no vices and went to Mass every Sunday. When we graduated in March, I said goodbye and did not see him for almost a year—at the frozen Chosin.

Somehow, Joe recognized me with all that cold weather equipment on. I was so surprised to see him with a big black cigar hanging from his mouth, and every other word he spoke was filth. He pulled out a bottle of whisky and offered me a drink. What a change in a person in such a short time!

We talked about his sweetheart and that car he had talked about in boot camp. It was some model of a Buick that he was saving money for. He said he was going to marry his loved one when he got back. I said goodbye as my outfit started moving out. It would be three years before I would see Joe again at Camp Pendleton.

After the hand shaking and all that, I asked Joe if he married his sweetheart, and his face clouded up. He said "Come on, I'll buy you a drink and tell you the whole story." He started by asking if I remembered that car he was going to buy, I said yes. He then told me that when he took his bride to be to the theater there was slush snow on the road. A big truck went racing by and threw slush all over his car. He rolled down the window and started hollering every curse word he could think of. His sweetheart was shocked. She could not believe what her loved one had just said. Joe knew he had made a mistake.

He waited until everything had a chance to settle down, and he leaned over, took her hand, and said, "I'm sorry honey, no shit." There would be no wedding, and Joe would end up marrying the Corps. He made sergeant major and was one hell of a Marine.

Staff Sgt. Peda was my drill instructor. He was an Indian and the toughest SOB I had ever met. He had fought at Iwo Jima, where he was wounded, and received the Silver Star. There was a whore in the nearby town named Ruby he would go to see on liberty. Sometimes he would come back loaded, and I hated it when this happened and I was the fire watch.

The first thing he would do was to call the fire watch. I had heard a lot about drunken Indians, and I held my breath as I went running to the drill instructor's office. He would start by telling me about Ruby and ask me about my general orders. What a relief when he told me to go back to my post. I always remember when he told me, "Canada, if I see you on the battlefield with your guts hanging out, I'll stomp on you."

I came across him wounded by a burp gun. He had taken three slugs across his gut, but he was holding his stomach and walking to the first aid station. We got him to lie down on a stretcher and took him to the first aid station. He was loaded in a small airplane, and as we watched, it took off but could not climb high enough and crashed into the side of a mountain.

We climbed up, and both he and the pilot were still alive. We took them back to the airfield where they loaded them into a cargo plane, and this time it made it. It would be many years later that I ran into now Master Sgt. Peda. I was a staff sergeant, and we had to inventory the staff NCO club. He told me he was retiring and planned to live in Japan. I wished him luck, shook his hand and wished him a safe trip.

I became a drill instructor in 1955. There was no series supervisor. This was before the McKeon event happened at Parris Island. In my last book, "We Few, We Chosin Few," I included the story what happened to McKeon. After DI School, I was sent to the first Battalion for duty.

It was only because I had the training that later in life I could go to college and eventually write three books. For a boy who only had an eighth grade education, this was outstanding. I got a high school equivalent as a DI. When I went to college, I was on probation for the first semester. I received an A.A. at Mira Costa and went on to Pepperdine. My GI bill ran out just five units short of a bachelor's degree.

There were many trip wires for a DI, and of the class, I went through at DI School, only two of us made it for a complete tour of duty. Mistreating a recruit or taking money from one of them was a no-no. These two mistakes were the most common downfalls of the drill instructors. The money event usually happened when the recruits graduated. Each night a Marine was to put five dollars in the bucket. The right guide would take the money from the bucket and put it under the DI's pillow of his duty bunk.

Some other crazy events happened, and even today, it seems unbelievable. One DI had a girl friend who was a female Marine. They worked out a scheme wherein the woman would get in a large metal trash bin with metal doors on each end. The DI would march his recruits to the bin, and a recruit would jump in one door and have sex. As he got through, he would climb out the backside while a new recruit would take his place.

They were to split the money, but fate stepped in. The duty officer saw what was happening, and as he approached, everyone scattered. Just as he was to confront the woman, he got an emergency call. He secured the doors and went away. In the meantime, the trash truck arrived and picked up the trash bin and hauled it away to the dump.

Now the reader is expecting something bad to happen. Sorry—the truck came back with the woman sitting in the front seat. Her hair was full of trash, but otherwise she was OK. No one was ever punished for this.

The rifle range was at Camp Matthews. The recruits lived in squad tents. An all Indiana platoon joined the Marines together. In fact, there were two platoons. The senior DI, Staff Sgt. Brunton, was also from Indiana.

I think I am the only person since the "War Between the States" that flew the stars and bars over U.S. government land. This was before the McKeon deal. Today I would have been busted and put in the brig. All the Marines back then were white.

I would fall the recruits in and have them hoist the colors up while saluting and singing Dixie. As you can see in the picture, the flagpole was over 16 feet tall. They would lower the flag at sunset. I did this the whole schedule while at the rifle range.

The two platoons graduated and went back to Indiana. They had a big parade in their hometown.

Picture 4 – Camp Mathews

The greatest satisfaction for a DI is when the troops graduate. That playing of the Marine Corps Hymn as they pass in review causes one's heart to beat with pride. I do not know how many DIs get a letter from one of their troops telling them how much the training helped them. I received not one, but two calls, then letters, from troops that I trained.

Over 40 years had passed. My wife and I had attended a reunion at Camp Lejeune, and when we got home, there was a message from Roger Galassini in Chicago trying to get in touch with his drill instructor from the Marine Corps. I called him, and a few days later, he wrote me a letter:

Dear Sgt. Canada

Thanks for the telephone call. The day I transferred to a mustering out company, I boarded a base bus, and you were aboard. We talked a bit. The first day we went on schedule, you and Staff Sgt. Brunton picked us up. Therefore, you were one of the first and last persons I met as a Marine.

When we went to chow that first night, you marched us. Afterwards you assembled us, told us to stand at ease, and lit the smoking lamp. You asked us if we knew Sgt. McKeon; some did, most did not. You told us his story and said we had decision to make. If you trained us as the way the word was coming down, we would be no better than dog face soldiers; or you could train us as you had others, and if we made it, we would walk out as Marines. Of course, we bought into your training. What impressed me in later years, when I thought about what you had done, was first you asked us to look from the forks down two roads; one easy, one hard; one results OK, the other better. Secondly, you put your stripes on the line because of how you defined yourself and the Corps.

Well, I went from being a dropout kid to returning to college and law school. When I retired I was running a company listed in the NYSE. During that career, there were rough spots. When I faced that fork and had to make a call that was when I thought of you: "What would Canada do?"

Sometimes people will say that I was lucky, and my response is always, "It was not luck; it was the Marine Corps." It is fitting that I am writing today, November 10. Happy Birthday (Marine Corps Birthday).

The day that our platoon photo was taken, you were absent. So may I impose and ask you to please send a photo of yourself?
Roger Glassini

Picture 5 – Smokey the Bear

Before the McKeon incident, we wore utility and barracks caps on the drill field. It was not too long after that event that the Smokey the Bear cover became the uniform of the day. The Marine Corps had a troubleshooter that came to San Diego. He was Lt. Gen. Alan Shapley. He got all the drill instructors in the theater and told them how the Marine Corps was going to change. This was when they brought in the series supervisor, an officer in charge of the training.

The general asked if there were any problems, and one DI got up and said that the barrack cover was too hard to run in. The general asked if everyone agreed. To the man, everyone said, "Yes, sir." The general looked at his watch and said, "It is now eleven o'clock; at twelve o'clock the uniform will be piss covers" (overseas covers). Not too long after this the Smokey, the Bear cover was the uniform of the day.

The second recruit's name was Jim Bruncher, and he was in my first honor platoon. He was from Waterloo, Iowa.

11

Picture 6 – My First Honor Platoon

Dear Sgt. Canada,

This is mostly a test email to be sure it finds you. Hearing your voice on the phone was simply unbelievable. After all these years, who would believe it could happen? Indeed, there has been a lot of water over the dam of our lives. Lord knows what has become of the men of platoon 127 MCRD that I graduated with; some are no doubt in their final resting places. I would not ramble on about my past but share with you on another day. Again, thank you so much for allowing me to visit you today. In closing would like to say that your leadership skills as a DI made a lasting impression on me and enabled me to face most obstacles in life.

Semper Fi
Jim Bruncher

Sgt. Richard was one of the best DIs I ever knew. I worked with him when I first became a DI, and he taught me a lot. I never forgot one of his tricks to teach a recruit never to call his rifle a gun. When a recruit called his rifle a gun, he was made to hold his rifle above his head in his right hand and grab his cock in his other hand and double time around the platoon yelling, "This is my rifle, this is my gun; this is for fighting, this is for fun." It was a good lesson, and usually this taught all of them.

One time after we graduated our platoon, we took off and went to Mexico. We were locked up in jail because Richard had to stop in an alley to take a leak. There was a Mexican standing there with a large topcoat on. He asked Richard for some money, and when Richard refused, he asked where we were from, and Richard told him the Mexican word for Texas. He pulled back his topcoat and pulled out one of the longest pistols I have ever seen and told us we were under arrest. A paddy wagon soon came and hauled us off to jail.

Years later when I was taken in a scam involving my son, I remembered how filthy the jail was, and this helped pull the scam off on me. There was urine all over the floor and lice crawling all over the place. Not only this, but there was a gang that jumped on us and took everything we had. I did not start fighting until they tried to take my wedding band. It was this event that got me out of jail the next morning. When I started fighting, everyone that was on Richard let him go, and jumped on me. They were choking me, and I decided that the ring was not worth my life, so I let it go. They were about to take Richard's shoes off when I started fighting, and he had hid the money in his shoes that got me out the next morning.

I was thinking of this when I thought of my son, Patrick, being locked up in Spain, and I ended up losing $10,000 in a scam. I will talk about the scam in a later chapter, but I want the reader to remember the conditions of this jail and know why I fell so easily.

As good as Richard was as a DI, he was bad when it came to picking a mate for life. He met a woman Marine and fell in love with her. He married her and told me later that he only had sex with her one time. He came home one day and saw his clothes on the bed. She had taken all her coat hangers and left. When he caught up with her he told her he wanted a divorce, and she started crying. She was a Catholic, and they went to a priest and had the marriage annulled. Two weeks later, he saw her walking hand in hand with another woman. She had told him that she was a lezzie. Like many Marines, old Rich just faded away.

From time to time I go to the MCRD and watch the recruits graduate. One thing has changed since I was a recruit and a DI: the giving of Marine Corps emblems. Now, upon graduation, each Marine is given this hard-earned emblem. The pride upon receiving it is very emotional.

While I was on the drill field, they made the movie "The DI" in 1956. Jack Webb used everyone in the movie who was a Marine except one. I was interviewed for a part, but a gunny sergeant got the part as the hillbilly. The Marines could not be paid for their part but were given watches with "The DI" inscribed on the back.

Picture 7 – Author

This is a picture of me before I joined the Marines. In fact, I wore this outfit when I went to Parris Island. The woman's circle gave this suit to me for Christmas, 1948, and everything that is not Marine Corps issue was either sent home or given to a homeless place. I was 17 and thought I knew everything. How little did I really know?

Chapter Three

From Camp Lejeune to War

Checking in for duty after my boot leave, I was assigned to shore party. This outfit set up the beach equipment so everyone knew where the ammo, rations, fuel and other supplies went. They had a small red patch on the outside of their uniform on their leg so they would be easy to identify.

It was late March 1950, and it would only be about three months before the war in Korea started. I mostly stood guard duty and cleaned the equipment. One day they were looking for anyone who wanted to try out for track. I had never run track but was very fast in football; so I said I wanted to try out. They tested me and put me down for the 440-yard run. In the trial heat, I started out fast, and three quarters around the track, I slowed down and came in second.

There were a couple of runners who saw me and told me to watch them and that they would tell me when to break for home. I started out in the pack, and about halfway the first guy gave me the sign to pick up the pace. Close to the finish line the other guy gave me the sign to let it all out. I won the gold medal. I thought this was the beginning of a new event, but the war started, and so much for my new adventure.

The Marine Corps on paper had two divisions: first Division was at Camp Pendleton, California, and second Division was at Camp Lejeune, North Carolina. In reality, if you were to take both divisions and all ship and shore stations and put them together, you would still have one incomplete division. In the Seventh Marine Regiment, there were reserves that made up most of that regiment at the Chosin.

The first thing the Marine Corps did was to load up the second Marine Division on troop trains and transport them to Camp Pendleton. It was one crazy trip with stops in Alabama and Texas. We only did exercises in Alabama station, but it was a very large turnout, and a large crowd was on hand to see the event.

In Texas, however, they let the troops into the train station and blocked off all exits. It was funny to see so many horny Marines down on one knee trying to get the Mexican girls to marry them. I would have given a month's pay to hear some of their lines. Going to war does funny things to men.

Over 60 years have passed since I went on that train and stopped at the bottom of Rattlesnake Canyon. Most of the railroad track has long since gone. Where we stopped, however, there is still track, but it has palm trees growing up between the rails. I still feel sorry for the porter for one of the events that happened. We collected only two dollars and 32 cents, and I will never forget the look on his face. We were a little embarrassed, but no one had any money, so such is life.

Camp Del Mar was west of U.S. Highway 101, and in those days you could walk across the road and hitchhike to L.A. or any of those places we thought all the movie stars would be. My friend Mike and I wanted to go to L.A. As we stood with our thumbs out a young couple stopped, and when we told them where we wanted to go, they said it was not too hot. They added that they were going to a beach where Stan Kenton was playing. As an old country boy, I had never heard of this guy, but we went along with the idea and got to sit onstage while the band was playing. I must say that the music was not what I was used to, but the singer was a knockout.

So much has changed since 1950. The old Highway 101 is no longer. It has been replaced with Interstate 5. Trying to walk across this now is not a good idea. There is also a coaster railroad that will take you to San Diego. It will turn around here in Oceanside and will take you east to a couple of towns along Highway 78 as well. They changed the 101 to be called the Coast Highway. The only thing that even referred to the 101 is a small restaurant called the 101 Cafe.

THE 101 CAFÉ. A flashback to the 1950s and 1960s and the Beach Boys, the 101 Café is an Oceanside landmark as well as a popular place to eat.

Picture 8 – 101 Café

Only a couple of days went by before we started loading the ships. We worked without relief in a 12-hour shift. They were feeding us four meals, but soon the troops were falling asleep anywhere they could find a spot. This went on for a couple of days; then they loaded us aboard ship. I fell asleep, and when I came to, we were far out to sea.

I had never heard of Dramamine so it did not take long before I was seasick. Years later I learned the secret, but that first trip made me wish I was dead. When we got to Kobe, Japan, the first bar I went to only had three American records, and I wanted to break the one that was called, "I'd Like to Get You on a Slow Boat to China."

The old uniform worn in the field was called herringbone. It was made into an old salt outfit by tying it on to a rope and dragging it behind the ship for a couple of hours. This would turn it slowly into a white-faded color. We boots would do anything to look like we had been around for a while.

We marched to an old Army base that was all Quonset huts except the gym. The gym saved many lives when the typhoon hit. Early we had to reload the ships for combat and get them out to sea before the storm. I had the bad luck to be walking post when the typhoon hit. The tin on the huts started flying through the air. I was hanging on to the fence to keep from getting blown away, and the tin was flying around cutting the electrical wires, which started fires around the area.

I remember I had just put on a fresh khaki uniform, and now I looked like a drowned rat. I slowly worked my way to the mess hall. The noon meal was still on line, and nobody was there. The only thing I can tell the reader about the food was what they had for dessert: It was butterscotch pudding. I took one of those big serving spoons and started eating. To this day I cannot eat that stuff.

A couple of days later they had a formation and started calling out names and to fall into a line to the left. My name was called, and they told us we would not be making the landing because we were too young and had to be 18. All of us were 17. What a letdown.

No liberty had been allowed, but many guys climbed over the fence, and it was quite funny to see them coming back drunk and the Marines on post helping them back over. At this time, nobody had ever been on the outside.

The outstanding memory was of a Japanese girl, who was handicapped with speech and hearing problems, coming to the fence with a dog and giving oral sex through the fence. There was a long line, and she was doing it free. If it had happened in our country, maybe they would have given her a medal or something for aiding in the war effort.

The troops moved out, and those who were left took over guard duty. We had a lot of stuff left in the warehouses on the docks. There were PX supplies, personal items that could not be taken into combat, items like locker boxes and sea bags. I remember months later when I went home that they could not find my sea bag and gave me a complete new issue.

We finally got liberty, and this was where I heard that record about the slow boat. It is also where I lost my virginity. Back at Camp Lejeune, a group of hot-to-trot guys went to Jacksonville to a cathouse for sex. Of course, I was a virgin, but like most young guys, I never told anyone. I think the price was $5, but as I waited, I saw they had only three girls and that they were all fat and ugly. I went in and told the girl that I did not want to do it but stayed long enough to tell everyone what a great time I had. Life is full of disappointments, and this was one.

Picture 9 – Marines Kids in Kobe, Japan

The Inchon landing was on September 15, and I did not turn 18 until the 30th. My life in Japan was a great experience, but they loaded us up and sent us on to Korea.

The picture above is of some of those 17-year-old Marines that were at Kobe. On the far right is a kid named Flannary who went to the same outfit as me at the Chosin and lost both feet to frostbite. I never saw any of the others again. These kids would have been either juniors or seniors in high school.

Due to heavy casualties, I would not be going back to shore party. The 5th and 7th Marine Regiments both lost a lot of men, so we were shipped to the 5th as replacements. I had always wanted to be a fighting Marine, and the 5th would have been my first choice. My new outfit was H-3-5. I was placed in a 6 mm mortar outfit as an ammo carrier.

As we were flown in I could see snow on the ground, but until they opened the door I could not tell how cold it was. It was so cold that I had a hard time taking a deep breath. Oh my God, what had I gotten into?

I had on long johns and my winter service greens, a heavy parka and mittens, and I was freezing. The boots would prove to be inadequate, and the felt inserts had to be replaced often. The big problem was the gloves. They were mittens with a trigger finger. To unlace the boot one had to take the glove off, and when this happened your hands would freeze. Everyone had two pairs of felt inserts, and when you replaced the one you were wearing, you would put the one you had taken off under your armpit to dry out. With all the clothes we had on, you can see how crazy it was.

A sergeant came and took me to an open field. He pointed to a telephone pole about 800 yards away and told me to zero in on it. I fired a few rounds and then was given a field of fire in case of an attack. I tried to dig a foxhole, but the ground was frozen, and my entrenching tool just bounced off the soil. I piled all my equipment in front to get some protection from enemy fire and climbed into my sleeping bag with all my clothes on. It was so cold that soon I was freezing. After several hours someone came and took me to a warm-up tent. My left foot had frozen to my boot, and as I took the boot off, the pain was almost unbearable. I put dry felt inserts in both boots and slowly pulled the boots back on. It was this effort that saved my feet.

All night long I heard firefights, but no one came through my line. It was the longest night of my life, and I was so happy to see the sun come up the next morning. Someone came and took me to my new outfit, H-3-5. I was put in a 60 mm mortar section; I did not know the first thing about this weapon. They made me an ammo humper. They had an ammo bag that fit over your head with pockets in front and back to carry the ammo. There were high explosives and white phosphorous rounds that we had to carry. The range chart said the max range was 1875 yards,

Today the same weapon goes twice as far, around 4000 yards. I saw a demonstration at Camp Lejeune and thought how much we could have used that range in Korea. The weapon is made of a different material and lighter.

The one event that was a real tragedy was the ambush of task force Drysdale. Before the breakout of the reservoir a convoy of about 800 Americans and British Marines were sent to the farthest Marine stronghold of Hagaru-ri. The convoy was named after the highest ranking officer who was a British Marine, Col. Drysdale. There were a few tanks at the head of the column, but the road was small and unpaved, and when one tank was knocked out, the whole convoy was brought to a standstill. The Chinese cut the convoy in half, and before long they cut it again, making it many small seconds before it was finally overcome. Those who made it to Yadam-ni were some of the British Marines and Marines from G Company.

Over 600 Marines were either killed or captured, making this one event stand out as losing more troops captured than at any other time during the war. Most of these were headquarters and non-combat Marines. They also had the mail meant for Christmas of 1950.

We soon found out we were making a breakout back to the sea. We would first clear out the Chinese from our present position to Hagaru-ri. There we would re-supply and fly out all the wounded and bring in replacements.

We were told that all equipment except our weapon, sleeping bag and ammo was to be turned in and destroyed. We ammo carriers were to pick up additional ammo for the attack. There would be no re-supplies until we reached Hagaru-ri.

We sat around all day eating and drinking juice from the mess hall, which would also be destroyed. I had a large can of frozen tomato juice, and I kept putting it on the fire, then drank the juice until I reached the frozen part, then back on the fire until it was empty.

The reader must know that everything was frozen and that without heat you could not eat anything. The hero for everybody was the tootsie roll and a hard candy called Charms. Without them I do not think many would have made it out of the Reservoir. Once I tried to eat frozen beans and got such a stomachache that I had to stop.

A day or two before we moved out I was watching an air strike on the hills in front of our position, when one of the airplanes was hit. A long tail of black smoke trailed behind the plane as it slowly started losing altitude and tried to land on a small air strip just in front of me. It was made for observation planes and too small for this aircraft. The plane had already used up most of the strip when it crash—landed in the rice paddy at the far end. This was one lucky young naval officer because the plane did not catch fire, and it landed upright. Other than being cold, he was all right and soon out of this area.

Chapter Four

The Breakout

Because the enemy held all the surrounding high ground, we waited until dark before we made our move. At first it was start and go; then we slowly picked up the pace. This would go on until we hit a roadblock, and then we had to fight our way clear. Every bridge was blown and had to be dealt with.

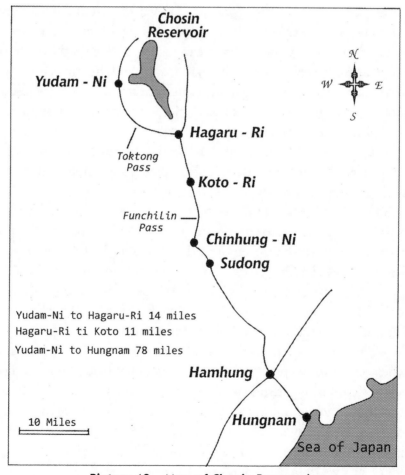

Picture 10 – Map of Chosin Reservoir

From Yudam-Ni to Hagaru-ri, it was 14 miles. It would take the 5th and the 7th Marines 79 hours to break through to Hagaru-ri. I can still hear the cheering as we marched through the gates singing the Marine Corps Hymn. Our beloved Gen. Smith was wiping the tears from his eyes. We must have looked like a crazy group of wild animals. We got our first hot chow in quite a few days: all the pancakes you could eat.

It is hard to believe that Washington had written off the Marine Division as a lost cause. Earlier, when the Marines were building the two airstrips, Gen. Almond wanted to know what the reason for them was. Now he knew as he flew into the improvised airstrip at Hagaru-ri. He wanted the Marines to have an escape route to the sea leaving all their gear behind. This man just did not know what we Marines were made of. I was proud when Gen. Smith gave the negative answer and said we were going to come out as Marines. This included all our weapons and equipment.

I could not help but think that earlier, as we were fighting our way to the Yalu River, they said we would be home for Christmas. Now I was thinking that we would be damn lucky to get out of this trap alive. That song, "What a Difference a Day Makes", was very true.

On the breakout we had to relieve Fox Company at Toktong Pass. Capt. Barber was the CO, and they had held out for five days with heavy losses. Later he would receive the Medal of Honor, and they would make a movie about this outfit. Also the leader of the outfit that was to break through the Chinese surrounding Fox Company got the Medal of Honor.

This pass was over 4,000 feet and was the main terrain feature that both we and the enemy knew was the key to breaking or holding the movement.

There was one piece of action wherein we made an attack to the right flank while leaving Yudam-Ni. We set up our 60 mm guns in a draw, got the range and fired off a WP (white phosphorus) round. We got an adjustment and fired off the second round. Then we got the command to fire an HE (high explosive) round. There was a telephone wire above the number three gun that no one had seen. The round hit this wire, and it wiped out the whole gun crew.

I was bending over removing a round from the canister when the explosion happened. Luckily I had my sleeping bag on my backside, and it took up most of the shrapnel, which went clean through the bag and wounded me on my right side buttock. It was so cold that it stopped the bleeding, and with a small dressing I was able to help get the rest of the wounded to an area where they could be treated.

Not too long after this I was standing behind a machine gunner firing over his head to the area where we were receiving heavy fire. The gunner was in the prone position firing, when suddenly I saw rounds stitching the ground, and he was hit. I was standing over him with my legs apart and watched as the rounds plowed up the ground between my legs. This was one lucky day for me.

Those beautiful F4U Corsairs came on station, and soon they wiped out the unit that was firing at us. You could see and then hear those machine guns tearing up the area. Then another passed, and I watched the napalm as it tumbled from the aircraft and became a big fireball when it hit the ground. If there was one thing that made a difference on the breakout, it was the air cover, but sometimes due to the weather we could not get it. I'll always remember this aircraft and think that it was the best of all times.

Some say the temperature was 24 degrees, and some say it was 40 below and the wind chill facture around 75 below. All I can say is that it was damn cold and let it go like that. The equipment we were issued was not up to standard, and many men did not make it home because of it.

The night we spent at Hagaru-ri was one of taking six parachutes and putting them on top of each other for a shelter. There was a large airdrop before we arrived so there were parachutes everywhere. We were not smart enough to outdo Mother Nature, for when we awoke the next morning we were covered with snow. It just sifted through all that silk.

We had to pass through the ambush that was named after Drysdale. Many have written what they saw and what they felt as we passed through. In one truck there were two Marines who were the only ones who still had their clothes on. All the other Marines were completely naked. The two were sitting, and in one Marine parka was a small puppy with his head sticking out, dead (all our Marines were dead and the Chinese had stripped the others for their clothes for their own warmth).

On the surrounding ground, was the mail meant for our Christmas. As the wind blew you could see letters tumbling across the rice paddy. Would you believe that one Marine actually found a package with his name on it?

There was a very young Chinese dead wearing a dress blue uniform that had belonged to a US Marine Sergeant Major.

Of all the naked Marines one stood out, and I still get a little emotional when I think of him. I wrote a poem that was published in my last book that I read to high school students each year on Veterans Day. He, of course, was naked and sitting up against a truck tire with his hand held out with his palm up like he was asking for something. The sun had come out, and the warmth had melted the ice in his eyes, and tears were running down his cheeks. I had a hard time holding back my own tears, he was so young.

I remember one area that we came upon, a unit of Chinese all standing in their holes, frozen. They had rushed around the Marine column and in doing so worked up a sweat. The sweat froze them. (I remember years later when they discovered an army of Chinese with their horses, buried. That was the army of some emperor of the past. All the expressions on those man-made faces were the same as those now frozen.) There was no expression of pain, hate or any other that would give one a clue as to their last thoughts.

There was another firefight I cannot forget. We moved through a now destroyed village. The Chinese had hidden under the building, and after we passed they came out firing at us. We had a tank nearby, and upon seeing what was happening, we opened fire and wiped all the Chinese out. Not one Marine had been killed, only three wounded.

I must confess that by the time we got to Kot-Ori, my mind was pretty much out of it. I remember that it was very crowded, and we did not stay there too long. I do remember that before we got to the Funchilin Pass we passed large sections of burned-out trucks and dead Marines, some still on their machine guns as though they were waiting for the next attack. I made a bad mistake that could have cost me my life. I opened one of the doors of a burned-out truck and saw several grenades on both the floor and seat that had the pins already pulled. As I slowly closed the door I said, I'll never do that again.

Picture 11 – Star of Koto-Ri

The star of Koto-Ri was an early Christmas present from God to the first Marine Division. There was a combat correspondent by the name of Sgt. Richard Holtgraver. He wrote a beautiful story about the Star of Koto-Ri. In it he described how important this event was to the survival of the 1st Marine Division. He wrote how this battle would become one of the greatest battles in American military history: the battle of the Chosin Reservoir.

A heavy snowstorm started around dusk. Without clear weather the Air Force could not drop the equipment needed to repair the bridge. It would take another two days with the temperature way below freezing and the wind chill factor around 70 degrees below.

The storm was still in progress on December 8, and it did not look good. Without clear weather the Marines were stuck and would not to be able to get all their equipment out. As Richard wrote, just when all hope had vanished a faint little white dot could be seen through the falling snowflakes just before 2200 hours. It was the star that became known as the Star of Koto-Ri That small object caused such excitement that we begin singing the Marine Corps Hymn. I do not think there was a dry eye in the whole base. That Star of Koto-Ri would become the Chosin Few logo in 1983. That star meant we would be able to complete our mission.

That is why you see the letters in the star CF; this stands for the Chosin Few. The tiny lone star in a cloud-filled sky gave hope to Marines just when they needed it the most. On December 6 the whole first Marine Division was at Koto-Ri. They had one obstacle left in the way for clearance to the sea: the destroyed bridge at the Changjin Power Plant.

Of all the action that we had getting to the Funchilin Pass, there was nothing more exciting than crossing over the tread way span that had replaced the bridge the enemy had blown up. Those spans were not too wide, and with the wind blowing pretty hard from the north, I must admit that saying the Lord's Prayer was on my lips. Looking down, there was about a 1500 foot sheer drop.

Years later when I was making static line parachute jumps of 1250 feet, I remembered that this was still closer to earth than that walk across the bridge.

To get those spans in they had to be dropped by parachute. They had dropped eight spans; one had been destroyed, one captured by the Chinese, so six would have to do the job. I learned years later that those spans were too short, and they had to fill in the space with frozen Chinese bodies and packed snow. There were tanks that did not go over the bridge. They sent an air strike to destroy them along with the bridge the next day.

We had some Chinese prisoners who were moving along in our column. I remember one poor soul who had no footwear, and his feet were frozen. Each time he put down his foot you could hear a dull thump. But he did not stop. There were so many tragic events that I think God was not there to take care of them.

At the bottom of the pass we were told there would be a truck along soon to pick us up. We walked and walked along a frozen riverbed. Someone opened up with a machine gun. The tracers would hit the ice and do a crazy dance before they burned out. Someone got on the radio, and soon the firing stopped.

It seemed like forever before the trucks showed up. To get everyone in the truck we all had to stand. My feet hurt, and as the trucks would sway back and forth, someone would step on my feet. It is hard to express how much pain that was, but I would scream from time to time due to the pain. Then we were there. They had put up tents over an area that trucks had driven over and left deep ruts that now were frozen.

Each tent had a stove in it, and as we slept the ground slowly thawed out. We awoke the next morning deep in mud. It was so good to be warm that you could forget about that mud. I had almost forgotten what a pleasure it was to be warm.

Those British Marines were close by, and they were shaven and looked like they were here all along. Their morale was high, and it made me stick out my chest and get squared away. Life was worth living once more.

The Marines have always taken pride in bringing out their dead and wounded. At the Reservoir we did bring out all our wounded and as many of our dead that was possible. Those left we buried in a mass grave. The hard part was picking up the dead and loading them aboard a truck. Some had died in positions that required breaking legs and arms just to load them aboard. There was a service and taps rendered at the gravesite, and all bodies were recorded.

I do not remember what ship we were loaded aboard; but the Fifth Marines and the rest was left of the British soldiers were on that ship. It was crowded, and they had to feed and sleep in shifts. It was a 24-hour-day job.

I went to the ship stores and bought several boxes of candy. One of the British Marines thought it was part of our ration and said, "I say, old chap, can I have a bit of sweets?" I laughed and gave him several bars of candy.

I cannot remember how long the trip was, but I do remember what happened to those dirty clothes we had worn for over a month. They were so dirty that the Navy took the handle of the broom and pushed them overboard. The long johns were so bad they were still standing at attention as they went in the sea. The smell was twice as bad.

One additional note of interest was the parka. It was a history of what one ate, blood, running nose and plain old crud all mixed together. In short, it would never have passed the board of health inspection. All in all, thank God. It looked like we were to have another day.

Chapter Five

Bean Patch to Punchbowl

I cannot remember how long that trip was from North Korea to Pusan. We were waiting for transportation around the dock when David Duncan, a famous war correspondent, started taking pictures. I was standing right alongside a kid who was sitting against a telephone pole with that 1000 yard stare. The picture he took became world famous. It was in Life Magazine.

I almost forgot about Maggie Higgins, another war correspondent who was interviewing some Marines. One of the questions she asked was, "What was the hardest thing you had to do?" One Marine said it was getting his prick out of all that clothing to take a piss. She got red in the face and walked away.

The trucks came and took us to a place that came to be known as the bean patch. There were squad tents with a stove in each tent. We were in reserve until we got replacements, and all we had to do was hold a fire watch. We passed part of the time playing cards, eating and sleeping. A lot of those Marines that came from Guam were going home.

Our corpsman was quite a poker player and won several thousand dollars. He told everyone about a car he would buy when he got back to the states. He made one mistake and went to play with some of his corpsman friends. They cleaned him out. Poor doc, he should have stuck with those dummy Marines. That car was now just another dream.

It was just a few days until Christmas. The mess hall was a short ways from our tent, so, like up north, the food froze quickly. You had to run back to your tent and put your mess kit on the stove to reheat it up before you could eat it.

On Christmas Eve we snuck over to the mess hall and stole some turkey legs. They were cooking the turkeys and all those other good things that one normally gets for this holiday. This would make up for Thanksgiving where everything froze at the Frozen Chosin. Where there was not a stove within a mile to reheat the frozen food.

Some of the replacements were reserves and had never been to boot camp. One Marine from the Windy City was so clumsy that he could never set up the mortar, and he was so out of shape that in the end they had to put him in the rear with the gear.

Soon we got our orders to move out. Holding police call we had a fire and burned all the trash. As we stood around the fire there was an explosion, and some kid hollered that he been hit. The corpsman came running over and saw red on the Marine's neck. He started wiping the blood away looking for the wound. He could not find a wound, and he smelled the red and found out that it was cherry jam. Everyone started laughing, and the new kid got the nickname, The Cherry Jam Kid.

Our new mission was to search and destroy North Korean units that had been cut off when we made the landing earlier in the war. They were killing people from small villages and ambushing the UN troops. This action went on for a couple of months.

I remember one such mission when we were moving up a hill that had, at the top, a destroyed farmhouse. There was still snow on the ground that had melted part way so the ground was wet. We took a short break. Straw was all around the area, and usually one just dropped on the dry straw to get the max rest time.

Just as I was about to drop I saw some object sticking out of the straw. I removed some straw and saw a fuse of a 500 pound bomb. If I had sat down, the whole hill would have been blown away, and most of my unit would have been killed. We called for a bomb disposal Marine who was attached to our unit. He waited until we got a safe distance away. When the bomb went off it blew away half of the hill. God was with me.

Our company was out in front of the division for over three months. We had nothing but C-rations. They were good, but anything can soon get boring. I wrote my dad, who was in the veteran's hospital, and asked if he could send me something else. One of the Red Cross women went out and bought a package that had such things as pancake mix, canned bacon and other canned goods that would not spoil.

When the package arrived there were four boxes of pancake mix along with many other goodies, which I gave to those ammo humpers to carry in the bag along with the ammo. These caused troubles because those boxes started breaking open after some time, getting the pancake mix all over the ammo. The lieutenant was not too happy.

During the Korean War the C-rations came in a box that had three meals for the day. This was OK, but there was only one plastic spoon. When we got through the meal we would put the spoon in our top pocket until the next meal. This became a health problem as everyone would come down with dysentery. It took a long time before they solved the problem. The new rations came in a box with one meal and one plastic spoon.

Before the new rations came out, there were good things to be said about the old C-rations. Everyone liked the ration that had beans and franks, pound cake and peaches. The first one always got that ration. There was a ration that nobody wanted: the one that had meat and beans, meat and noodles and the fruit was apricots. I remember one time we were on a steep mountain when we got our rations. By now we had a way to make it fairer. We would turn the box upside down and shuffle the rations. It was lucky to get the right one. You would soon know who got the bad ration. First you would hear the holler then see those rations flying over the mountainside.

Strange things always happen in a war. Now we had Korean laborers bringing our rations up the mountain. Somehow the word got out that those Koreans loved the meat and noodles and would trade sardines for them. You would no longer hear that yell but sheer laughter.

Like someone had just won in bingo. In my last book I wrote a poem called "The C-ration Shuffle." That told just the way it was.

They were using the Marines like a fire brigade. When they got a break in the lines they would send in the Marines to plug it up. One day this all black army unit was hit by the Chinese, and they broke and ran. They left their weapons and all their gear. As we were going up to plug the hole, we ran into that unit streaming down the road, yelling like wild men. In their eyes you could see sheer terror, and they were saying to anyone who would listen, "Man, you all do not want to go there!" They could not get down that road fast enough.

The Chinese had held the area they had left before they were pushed back. The bunkers were made by the enemy, and they left bags of dried beans, knowing that they would return. We had beaten them so we had their supplies, and we would make good of them.

I was going to show off and cook up a mess of those beans. I put them in my helmet, added some water and started cooking. After three days those beans were still hard. I wrote another poem called "The Chef" that showed what a complete flop this was, but in the long run I did become a chef.

It did not take long before the enemy showed up. I was now the forward observer, and we had every key location plotted for a target. It was early morning and there was a little mist in the air. They came down the road double timing in formation, all of them wearing that padded winter uniform. There was a bend in the road as they came around the hill. We let them clear the hill, and then we opened with everything we had. Most of them were cut down where they stood.

Two ran across the rice paddy and made it under a small bridge. A machine gun opened up with short bursts and hit them in their feet. They slipped a little, and the gun would let loose another burst, and they would slip a little more. This went on for a short time before he killed them both.

Some tracers had set a few uniforms on fire, and being a little damp they smoked for a couple of days.

Most of our company was across the road to our right. It was here the Chinese attacked that night. They took heavy losses and found out the hard way that it was a Marine unit that kicked their butt. When they started their attack they started blowing bugles and that only made us all the more hostile.

We moved to an area that had a couple of native huts. We were told to dig in. It was raining and around midnight our foxhole filled with water. It was cold so we went to a hut that had a fire, but the place was full of smoke. You would run in, get warm and run out to get some fresh air. It was one sorry night. I had picked up a stick, and later I found out that it must have been poison sumac. At first, my hands got large blisters, and they become so large I could not get my finger in the trigger housing group of my rifle. Next my penis swelled up. It became such a problem that soon they sent me to a hospital.

Picture 12 – Chinese Battle

After the battle we moved through the area looking for anything that we could get some intelligence from. At the bottom of the picture above are a couple of dead Chinese troops. Just off the picture are quite a few more enemy dead. We had received heavy enemy fire and called up the tank that made short work of this roadblock.

At the hospital there had been an airdrop earlier. As soon as I could get up, we went looking for any canned goods that were not smashed. An F-80 fighter plane had crash-landed but was still intact nearby. We climbed up to look in the cockpit. Just as we left a kid reached down and pulled the handle that ejected the seat of the airplane. The explosive charge that ejected the seat killed him instantly. I left soon after this and returned to my unit.

Soon the summer offensive started. We were assigned a hill just off the main supply route. That night the Chinese started blowing those bugles and yelling. We had a hard fight and were almost overrun. It was back and forth, but we slowly got the upper hand and held on. The next morning they pulled us off the hill, and as we moved back we could see the Chinese on the other side of the valley running along the ridgeline trying to cut us off. A battery of 105 guns opened up on them, and soon there were not so many. It was almost point blank.

A point of interest was, as we were moving down the road, a P51 flew very low over our heads and made a victory roll, and it was a morale builder. We crossed the river and blew the bridge behind us.

We moved to a place called the Punchbowl. I would stay here until I got an emergency leave in December. My father was dying. By now I had been in the war for almost 18 months. The standard tour is around 13 months, so I had stayed longer than usual.

Picture 13 – Friends and Me

Andy Jackson, (far right) was wounded soon after this picture was taken and died on the hospital ship a short time later. Paul Gator Hymel (far left) was at a reunion in San Diego. In 2000 he had cancer and was in critical shape. I am in the middle.

In the morning, I walked down the hill and caught a 6x6 truck that took me to the rear. There was a large lounge chair in the back, so I plopped my skinny butt down and kicked back with a big smile on my face: I am going home.

The clothes I was wearing were a khaki army shirt, utility pants that were too short and a little ragged around the bottom and no cover. The way we got our clothes was when we got into Reserve, they set up a shower unit, and as you took off your dirty clothes and put them in the dirty clothes bin, you showered and went through a clean clothes bin and picked out something that fit you. That is how I got the khaki shirt.

I used to look for a shirt that had gunnery sergeant stripes on it. In the old days we had to stencil our stripes on. This could become a problem if you were promoted or busted—then you had to buy a new utility shirt.

Of course, in my case, some sergeant would see me with gunny sergeant stripes and make me block them out. I would end up with a big black square where the stripes had been. I had been wearing that steal pot(helmet) for so long that I do not remember when I lost my soft cover. The new ranks structure was made of metal that you put on your collar. This is still in use today.

Chapter Six

From Home to Discharge

My first night in Japan I was so tired that as I almost fell asleep, an older Marine came over to my bunk and said, "Hey, watch that guy across from you — he is queer." That woke me up. He had one of those big radios, and a bunch of Marines were around his rack drinking.

There was one Marine who like me had just gotten back from Korea. He was going back to the states because he had been selected for an officer's commission. The Marine who owned the radio kept giving that Marine more and more booze. The Marine who gave me the warning had been a cop in Chicago. He was on his way to Korea.

The "Do not ask, do not tell" that we have today (and soon to be changed) is in question, because, in the situation above, it would not have been a serious matter. The Marine from the Windy City just went and got the officer of the day who came and caught them in bed. They both were kicked out of the service.

Now, if this had happened in Korea in the front lines, it could have been more serious. At night there were usually two Marines in a foxhole, and sometimes there was a 50 percent watch. This meant that one Marine slept for an hour while the other was on watch. If there was either a woman Marine or a gay in that fighting hole, you did not have to be a rocket scientist to figure out what was going to happen.

If this did happen and no one was watching for the enemy, a lot of men could have been killed because someone had not done their job. Most of those who argue for gays being in the military they have never been in combat and do not know their ass from a hole in the ground. Maybe in the Army, Navy or the other branches of service where they are driving a truck or making bread, this life threatening action would not cause someone to die, but, brother, this one surely would.

The next morning we found bottles of booze under almost all the bunks, and I got a bottle of Jim Beam's black label to take home.

I was still wearing the same outfit the next morning and standing outside watching all the people coming to work. An MP jeep pulled up and told me that I was out of uniform and had to get off the street. I got mad and told those jerks that I had just gotten out of combat and these were the only clothes I had and that I would not get off the street for them or anybody else. They called the officer of the day, and soon he came driving up. He told me to get in his jeep and drove me to a supply depot where they issued me a complete new sea bag. It seemed that they could not find my old sea bag. This not only made me feel a lot better, but it made me a very proud Marine.

The airplane that took me to the states went the northern route, and we landed in Alaska. It was almost as cold as North Korea. All the buildings were connected, and they first took us to the mess hall. Then they took us to a barrack where we could sleep. After some time we were loaded aboard the aircraft, and we headed for Washington State, U.S.A.

When I joined the Marines I had taken out an allotment for my father. I was making $58, and I sent my Dad $50. This meant that I did not have enough money to get home. They sent me to the Red Cross.

I have heard a lot of bad things about the Red Cross, but they treated me very well. They bought me a ticket home and gave me enough money to eat. I have nothing but good things to say about them.

I stopped in Bethesda, Maryland, to visit the people who sent me clothes and Christmas presents while I was in the orphanage. It was pure luck that I did so because one of the families that I had stayed with when I visited them in 1948 was the Phillips.

Mr. Phillips was the vice president of the Virginia Railroad, and I told him I was going home because my father was dying, and I had 30 days before I had to go back to Korea. He took me to the Pentagon, and everyone there seemed to know him. He took me to a Marine Corps colonel and told him my problem. The colonel told Mr. Phillips to take me down to the cafeteria and get a cup of coffee and come back in a half hour.

I received new orders to Little Creek, Virginia, and for the first time in my life, I learned what having special pull meant. I was once more back in shore party, and in no time I made corporal and, shortly after that, sergeant. Hell, I had been a private first class for over two years.

I received my Purple Heart from Gen. Good. It was going good, and I got along with all the instructors. Soon they had me join the VFW. They gave me a job as bartender, so I made a little money on the side.

I am getting a little ahead of myself.

When I arrived in Norfolk, Virginia, I stopped by to see the Capps family. My old buddy Louis was about to graduate from high school. He was still going with his high school sweetheart Barbara Leclair. His sister Joanie, who I'd had a crush on most of my life, was dating a boy in the high school band.

I called my sister and told her I would see her tomorrow. She did not want to wait and said that she would be right over. Soon a station wagon pulled up, and it had a lot of girls and my brother in it. Billy was in the Army Airborne and had beaten me home.

Mrs. Childress (who drove the station wagon) was the woman who ran the foster home. After all the hugging and kissing, my sister told me they had a beach cottage and that was where we would spend the night. My brother caught me up on all the news and I learned that he was in love with a girl named Ann.

My dad passed away right after Christmas, 1951. We went to the VA hospital to claim his remains. His lawyer asked which one of us was Blackie, and I said it was me. He handed me an envelope that had over $2000 in it. It was all the money I had sent my father over the time I was in the Marines. We buried our dad in Lynchburg, Virginia. His brother Tom was buried there, and Uncle Tom's wife Bessie would be buried there later.

A year later around Christmastime my brother was out of work, and I played Santa for his six kids. (Both of his boys would join the Marines.) It was one of those deeds that the kids would never forget. I took Ruthie to the PX at Little Creek to do her Christmas shopping.

It was now around the end of my enlistment, but everyone had been given a year extension due to the Korean War which was still going on. I would only serve four months of this extension before I was discharged.

Before this I had a little accident and almost cut my finger off. They took me to the naval hospital in Portsmouth, Virginia, and gave me morphine. I did not know that I was allergic to it (it was years later that morphine almost killed me). Every time they gave me a shot I would start acting up.

One day while loaded on this drug I hit a nurse right between her running lights, and she went around for days with her eyes black. I felt guilty about it, but she forgave me. I made it up later, and she gave me a kiss as I left the hospital. Before I left, however, I got liberty and got in trouble once more.

All my clothes were in a sea bag and all messed up. I still had most of the money I had sent my dad, so I bought a new outfit. When I came back from liberty I was stopped at the main gate. They had a civilian cop on the gate, and he asked me if I was a patient at the hospital, and I said yes. He told me I was not allowed to wear civilian clothes. I said that I had a civilian clothes pass. He told me that it was not allowed at the hospital, so I was under arrest.

Something snapped inside of me, and I hit him with my hand that had been hurt. That knocked him out, but the pain I felt was almost unbearable. By now I was very angry, and I got inside the sentry booth. Soon the Marine guard unit showed up and told me to come out. I told them to get fucked, and they tried to force their way in. I kept hitting them with my cast, and it was taking its toll on them.

My doctor came down and told me to come out. He said no one would bother me. I asked if I had his word on it. He told me yes. As I left I gave a finger to those Marines who had tried to get me out. Next thing I knew they put me in a padded cell. They got me involved in occupational therapy. I was making things like leather craft and rugs. I made the nurse that I had hit a big rug with every color of the rainbow.

After going back to duty with the Marine Corp I got a discharge. Then I got a job working for C. E. Hobeck who owned an appliance store in Virginia Beach. I was still involved at the VFW, and my brother wanted to know if he could have his reception at the club. He was going to marry Ann. I soon found out that he had no money, and I ended up paying for the marriage license. One of the guys at the club owned some cabins on the beach, and I paid for a week's rental. I even ended up paying for their food. Now how in the Hell could anyone even think of getting married like this? This shows you what a crazy guy my brother was. It was a good thing that I loved him.

Another thing happened while I was working for the appliance store. I had to climb under a house to repair the plumbing. As I was working something bit me on the back of my neck. I got very ill, and if the guys at the club had not come to find out why I was not at the club,

I may have died. They took me to the hospital. The next morning when I got out, I quit my job.

I moved to Lynchburg and got a job with Jerry Farwell. His company repaired trucks and trailers. The pay was not too hot at Farwell, and I was having a hard time making ends meet. I had second thoughts about working there and leaving the Marines Corps. I joined the Marine Corp Reserves, after paying the rent, and a weekly bus pass I was broke. So I quit Jerry Farwell's.

I stopped to say goodbye to my cousin Little Bessie, and she slipped me $20. I hitchhiked to Richmond and after two days I was broke. I decided to go somewhere else, and while I was standing on a corner, an MG (that's a small sports car) pulled up and the driver asked if I wanted a ride. I asked where he was going and he said south. I said that it sounded good to me, so off we went.

He told me his name was Bob Thom and that he was from New Jersey. His family had a milk route, and he'd had an argument with his wife and took off. I soon learned that an MG was not made for sleeping. Sometimes we would stop at a roadside park to get some sleep. You were not too safe from the state police. They would make you move on. Sometimes we would sleep in a boxcar that was on the railroad siding. We ended up in New Orleans.

We took a job at a gas station. By pooling our money we rented a cheap apartment. It was not too long before we had hit rock bottom. Bob called home, and they sent him money to get back home on. I hated to see him leave because now we had become good friends. He left a note on the back of a picture of my sister that I still have. He said, "Do not forget to come and see me. You are the best friend I ever had." I never did see Bob again.

I was without a place to stay and not eating too well, so I went down to the Marine Corps Recruiting Station and asked to join up again. I was in the Reserves, so they told me I had to wait. I told the recruiter that I was broke, so they put me up in a hotel and gave me a meal ticket each day until my orders came in. This is just another good thing about the Marine Corps. They really take care of their own.

By now I had gotten to know this town like the back of my hand. When new recruits came in I would give them the tour, and they would supply me with things like sacks of Bull Durham tobacco. I got so good rolling a smoke that I could do it with two fingers. It did not take too long before I got my orders and was on my way back to Camp Pendleton, California.

Chapter Seven

Back in the Corps

It was another train trip back to California. This time I was sent to Casual Company at Camp Del Mar. This was where I started from on my way to war the first time. Casual Company is where they bring all those who re-enlist and those who are getting kicked out. I was about to meet some real charters whom I would get to know real well before we got to our new outfit.

It would be awhile before we got paid, and I only had the clothes I was wearing. They gave us light jobs to do while we were being processed. The Casual Company would be moved to the 5th Marine area in about a month.

Most of Oceanside has changed so much that it is hard to remember where everything used to be. Camp Del Mar was close enough to be able to walk downtown in a short period of time. The USO building has been gone a long time along with the Silver Dollar Bar where Moore and I had that fight. Even the Greyhound Bus station is gone.

Down near the beach a lot of high-rise buildings have replaced the amusement park. And the pier was rebuilt. The old Beach Lake Trailer Park has long since gone. A manmade harbor completely changed the landscape. Most people do not know what the old Oceanside used to look like. They think the harbor has been here forever.

In July, 1950, I met my first wife. Lorraine was working for the major newspaper in Los Angeles. We dated a few times, and every time I see the movie "From Here to Eternity," I remember that it was what we saw on our first date. I wanted to get married but she did not. She had two girls who were seven and eight years old, and she had just gotten over a bad marriage. Her first marriage was to a colonel in the Air Force, and he was paying child support. Nancy and Linda were the two girls' names, and we got along right away. I had orders for overseas and Lorraine came around. We got married at city hall in L.A. The picture below was taken right after we got married.

Picture 14 – My First Wife and Author

My new outfit was 3rd Battalion 9th Regiment 3rd Marine Division. I was still in the Reserves, so I shipped over for six years after I had been in Japan for six months. This meant that I could go home for 30 days on a re-enlistment leave.

Lorraine was living on Silver Lake Blvd. in L.A. when I left, and she now lived in Burbank. The girls loved riding horses so she had rented a home close to the stables. The school where the girls had started classes was to their liking. In short, everybody was happy.

My 30-day leave went by so quickly that all the many things that we wanted to do would have to wait. I was on my way back to Japan. We were scheduled to make a landing on Iwo Jima. It would be the first time any unit had been on the island since the battle in 1944, and it was loaded with duds. I forgot how many tons of duds that they had disposed of, .but still a number of Marines died.

It was a little chilly, and you could go into one of the many tunnels to get warm. We found many things like Japanese helmets, shoes and mess gear that told many silent stories. In the tunnels sulfur was rising with the steam, and sometimes it was hard to catch your breath. Along the shore the salvage crews were digging up whole landing crafts still loaded with the cargo of war.

I returned to the states early in 1955 and got orders to Lake Mead, Nevada. It was a top-secret base where they brought the A-bombs for testing in the desert. There was so much security that I knew it was not where I wanted to be. My wife did not like it too much either, and luck was on our side.

There was an order out looking for volunteers to go on the drill field. I volunteered and was soon on my way to San Diego. This would be one of the most important decisions I ever made. Without it, I would not be writing this book, and I probably would never have gone to college. In short, it changed my life and family for the better.

We located a home for rent in Pacific Beach. While I was going to Drill Instructor (DI) School, Lorraine got a job at Convair. She had been a secretary and was good at shorthand. She soon was an executive secretary.

Around this time Lorraine's ex-husband got in touch with her, wanting to pay a lump sum in order to stop paying child support. We agreed to a payment and soon bought a home in Pacific Beach a couple blocks from the ocean.

I bought my first and only dog. It was a boxer, and I named it after a statue at Parris Island: Sgt. Iron Mike. In those days there was no leash law, so you could take your dog on the beach. Today there are too many laws, and only some are for the better.

One day Iron Mike got hit by a car. The hospital was really expensive, so I found a home for him where he would be safe. I hated to see him go, but with all my time spent on the drill field, it was for the best.

I was assigned duty at the 1st Recruit Training Battalion. My first sergeant's name was Lepourt. He had been captured on Wake Island by the Japanese. I found out later that there were three more who had been prisoners from Wake. A point of interest was that the Marines had more people who made it through that tough ordeal than most of the other services. The Marines had always stuck together and took care of each other.

Being a DI is not the best life for a married man. You spend so much time with your platoon that you must have a wife who understands. So some marriages end up in divorce. The wife wants more, and the husband is not there for her support. However, one of those great satisfactions in life is when one sees his work was not in vain. They now can enjoyed that pleasure when their Marines pass in review for graduation.

Back in 1950 the Marine Corps rifle range was at Camp Mathews. (It is now at Camp Pendleton.) In those old days they would take the recruits by bus to Pacific Beach and march them up the hill with the cross that has been in the news for some time After a break they'd march down onto a dirt road to Highway 101, put a road guard out and cross over to the main gate of the base. The old 101 is now gone.

Today the base has been replaced with a veteran's hospital and a college on the other side of the old 101. Interstate 5 has replaced part of the old 101, and all the rifle ranges have been replaced with homes and shopping malls. There are a couple of places where, if you look hard enough, you can still see part of the firing lines.

When the recruit left the rifle range he was close to graduation. His hair had grown back in, and he was cockier than ever because he knew that the last part of boot camp would not be easy, but he could see the light at the end of the tunnel. That was all that mattered.

My tour was also about to end. Lorraine had learned that she had a rare disease called Scleroderma. The English meaning of the word was hardening of the skin. There was no cure, and we were told she had at the most about two years left. I could not believe this was happening, and she was speechless.

Soon she had to quit her job. Our home in Pacific Beach cost more than my pay alone could handle. We ended up giving back the house to the original owner. She lost the use of her hands first. The disease would progress inward to the internal organs, and eventually she would die. I left the drill field, and my new job was at Camp Pendleton.

The Marine Corps offered me a hard ship transfer back to San Diego, but I would not take it. I had to do something to keep from cracking up, so I went to 1st Force Recon. The training was hard, but I was in good shape due to having been a DI.

The Marine Corps had some problems when the first troops went to airborne school at Fort Benning. They started up a junior jump school at Camp Pendleton, and this corrected the problems before going to the Army for training. During World War II the Marines trained their own troops in parachute training.

The reason the Marines do not train their own troops in parachute school now was that, after the big war, there was a decision by the high staff in Washington, D.C. The Marines would be responsible for amphibious training, the Army for parachute training, and the Navy for ship and shore training.

Lorraine was Catholic, so getting divorced got her excommunicated. She was now trying to find some religion that would give her piece of mind. I tried to help, but she wanted to do it on her own. It was so hard sleeping with her. She was cold, and trying to give her comfort made it almost impossible for me to sleep at night. Her girls were a big help doing almost everything, including cooking, cleaning house and shopping. I was getting ready to go to jump school and so had very little time. We had been scheduled to attend three schools. The first course was basic jump school, which lasted two weeks. Jumpmaster and pathfinder team school were several weeks more. I hated being gone so long, but Lorraine's mother came down to stay with the kids and help Lorraine through her hard ordeal.

Chapter Eight

Recon Recon

Force Recon was a special unit. Like other special units in the past, it would be replaced by a new unit after it served a purpose. In the Second World War the Marine Corps had the Raider Battalion and a Parachute Battalion. Even these would be replaced as the war went on.

Force Recon was started up in 1967 when they combined the old amphibious recon and the new test unit to make up the company. It added to the new company a para recon platoon, a pathfinder platoon, an amphibious platoon and a headquarter section. The company commander would be Maj. Bruce Myers.

When we went to jump school there were 22 Marines in class. Upon graduation there was a physical competition between the two platoons—one, all the Marines plus army; the other, all army. It was, in reality, a test between the Army and the Marines. If the army did 100 push-ups, the Marines would double the count. The Army liked the Marines spirit but hated to be outdone.

Picture 15 – Graduation

The three schools we were to attend took place at two Army bases with most of the time spent at Fort Benning, Georgia. We graduated on October 10, 1957, and finished the last school, pathfinder school, on December 13, 1957, just in time for Christmas.

The 22 Marines were soon to be separated because they had formed up a new Force Recon company at Camp Lejeune, North Carolina. About half of the Marines who had made up the company would go east. Rebuilding a complete company would take time. There were a lot of volunteers, but most could not pass the physical. By now everyone had to go through a special school called junior jump school. I ran this school for about a year. We not only trained our own troops but all other units involved in parachute duties.

The pathfinder platoon was the queen of the ball. We got all the overseas tours and gave special shows for the likes of Chiang Kai-shek and SEATO (Southeast Asia Treaty Organization). The trips would take anywhere from two weeks to several months. It was the beginning of the tactics for helicopters and the combat deployment of them.

Our main transportation was the T-F aircraft, which could be launched from the aircraft carrier by a cat shot (catapult). Our pathfinder team was set up for 10 men because that was the max for this aircraft. Before we came along the main duty for this plane was carrying the mail to the fleet. The one drawback was a tail hook, which could be dangerous. We solved this problem by putting a burp (motion sickness) bag over the hook and taping it there before each jump.

When we returned from jump school, we had over a dozen jumps, all static line jumps from both fixed-wing aircraft and helicopters. The difference between jumping from fixed-wing and helicopters is that you have to go a little higher when jumping from the helicopter. It would be 1250 feet for fixed-wing and 1500 feet for the helicopter. By the time I left Force Recon, I had over 200 jumps

I only got hurt one time during a parachute jump. We were making a night jump, and I was carrying the radio. It was attached below the reserve parachute with two quick releases, both of which you had to release at the same time when you got close to the ground. It you did not, then one would get hooked up, and you ended up carrying it in. This was what happened, and I got my knee torn up.

We had attached to our leg a K-bar knife with a flare taped to it. The flare had on one end a smoke device used for daytime and a flare that is used for nighttime. One of the pathfinders came running over when he knew I was hurt. (The Marine's name was Rosa—he was killed in Vietnam later.) Rosa made a mistake and popped the smoke, which made the matter worse. In the end I went to the hospital and had a cast put on, which took me out of action for a while.

My second injury was not due to a parachute but caused by going up against a bigger man playing volleyball. I went up for a jump ball, and I was driven into the ground, landing on one foot and busting it. The big problem was that it happened in Taiwan, and I was the only jumpmaster.

We were to have a big show for a SEATO country, and there was no time to get a replacement. I went up because the show must go on. With my leg in a cast, I had to sit in the doorway of the aircraft with my legs hanging out and watch for the pilot to give the signal for the jump.

We came in at almost ground level, and just before the drop zone the pilot would haul back in the stick and get up to 1250 feet. He then threw two thirds on the flap, and as we hit the level I would give the signal to jump. This sensation is like being on an elevator when it stops at a floor level.

Because I was sitting in the doorway I had to flop on my back and roll to the rear of the plane for the troops to get out. All this was not bad; it was trying to pull in the deployment bags, that was the hard part. I had to get a good hold on the plane and pull with one arm, and if things went bad, I would be going out the door myself. The Chinese thought I was some kind of a hero and gave me that gung-ho thumb-up.

Picture 16 – Pathfinders and Rigger

The picture above is all pathfinders, except the parachute rigger, Carl Hinkle, who is on the back row, far left

There were operations wherein we operated off a carrier. The USS Princeton was one of the ships we used. There was an officer in charge of the pathfinder team. The enlisted men slept in one quarter, while the officer slept elsewhere. All the equipment was in the enlisted quarters, so when the ship speaker said for Pathfinder Team 32 to report to the flight deck on the double, this meant that I not only carried my radio but also the officers radio. It was a load.

You ran up to the flight deck, and there was a Marine pointing to a chopper all ready to clear the flight deck after you were loaded. No time was wasted, and the pilot knew where we were going ashore. We got in and did our job, and as soon as the operation was over they picked us up and took us back to the ship for future operations.

A pathfinder platoon had four teams, and this meant that we could provide four different landing zones. If it was a daylight operation we had four different color panels and four different call signs, so the helicopters knew which color they were assigned to. At night the panels were exchanged for color lights, and call signs could remain the same.

A pathfinder team had the assignment to jump in ahead of the landing force. They set up security, cleared any obstacles and set up communication. They blew up anything that might cause damage to the helicopter and hoped the landing force came in. We did have one machine gun to help suppress the enemy's fire. If for some reason the choppers did not make it, we were left holding the bag and had to get out the best way we could.

Force Recon would represent the Marine Corps every year at the California County Fair. I got this duty a couple of times. There used to be a store in downtown Oceanside called Kelly.

(It is also long since gone.) They would be good enough to loan us a couple of mannequins for the fair. We would put a wet suit on one and a camouflage uniform on the other.

We climbed to the top of the display building and tied the apex of the parachute to the cross beams. Then we would go to our sister services and start borrowing equipment, like two large fans from the Navy, a display case of all the ribbons and medals from the Air Force and some post and ropes from the Army.

The large fans we would turn upward to blow the parachute open, which was at the bottom, a mannequin in camouflage looking like a Marine making a parachute landing. The other mannequin wore a wet suit in a rubber raft making a landing on the beach. Out front of the display were the display cases and the ropes and post to secure the area.

Our sister services had all the latest up-to-date equipment for their display, but we would take the outstanding military display every year. On the backdrop of our display was a camouflage parachute and on the deck a couple of camouflage ponchos. We also had our weapons on display.

Thanks to our sister services, we would win with their help. The weapons had to be secured every night, so we were staying at the Air Force base while off duty. This event lasted about two weeks, and although it sounds like a lot of fun, it left one tired after it was over.

We did most of our operations from the airfield at Camp Pendleton, but sometimes we went to North Island for jumping from the TF Aircraft on a pre-dawn jump. I remember that it was damn cold in those hangers, and I was so happy to get aboard the plane. The picture is at Camp Pendleton, and the jumpmaster is checking my equipment. Notice the radio below my reserve chute. This is what I was carrying when I got hurt.

Picture 17 – Camp Pendleton

A couple of times in Okinawa we were invited to jump with the Special Forces. When jumping from the TF Aircraft the Marines had what is called a stick pusher. When we got the sign to go the stick pusher would push as hard as he could to get everyone out the plane as fast as possible.

The Special Forces had a drop zone where they would only put four men out on each pass. When we put 10 men out on the same strip they would not let us jump with them anymore. We did this so that upon landing we were close enough to form up quickly. They thought we were too reckless.

It was now 1959 and Lorraine passed away. The Catholic Church had a change of mind, and she was buried by them. Force Recon Staff NCO were the pallbearers at the funeral. They were a proud group of men, and I will never forget how proud I was. I will always be grateful for their services.

The rest of the company had their own schedule, but almost everyone was jump qualified. We also had cross training where, if there was an opening in different schools for swimming at UDT (under water demolishing team), we would send one who could make the school. There were Marines from all platoons who went to Ranger School at Fort Benning. Everyone had to go to both winter and summer courses at Bridgeport, California. The summer course was mountain leadership, and the winter course was cold weather training. There was also an NCO School where I would go when I left Recon and teach NBC(Nuclear, Biological, and Chemical) Warfare.

Below is a Para Recon team on an assignment for an operation called Blue Star taking place in the Philippines. The guy on the left went to jump school with me. His name is Leach.

Picture 18 – Para Recon Team

There was an operation in Japan where we were to be dropped on Mount Fuji. The weather was cold and wet. I would have called the operation off, but everyone wanted to jump, and against my better judgment we made the jump. Everyone landed OK except one who landed on the tent of the aggressor and went through the tent, to the surprise of its occupier.

It was then we learned that the operation had been called off. We had a hard time trying to start a fire. Everything was wet, and even using the flare to start the fire took some doing. We huddled around trying to get warm, but it was almost a waste of time. We spent almost the whole day before we got transportation back to the ship.

We then only had enough time for a meal and a change of clothing before we loaded aboard a truck that drove us all night to a Marine Corps airbase. All our parachutes were wet, and the base had a loft where we could hang them to dry. They then had to be repacked. We had a parachute rigger who went with us on most of our trips. I left Force Recon in 1961. Like all good things, there is always an end.

Chapter Nine

From 3rd Battalion, 3rd Marines to Vietnam

I joined the 3rd Battalion 3rd Regiment 3rd Marine Division, and when I went overseas, Lt. Col. Stormy Sexton was the commanding officer. Years later when my kids were in high school, Stormy was in charge of the ROTC program at Oceanside High. Looking back on my 20 years in the Marine Corps, he was the best commanding officer I ever had. Back in those days our tour was 13 months. This war has not shortened the tour.

During that time you would spend aboard ship about three months. It was called the afloat phase, and usually we would have a port of call at Hong Kong, the Philippines and other ports there was time for. Hong Kong was a great liberty port when the British were in charge. You could buy everything your heart desired.

The 3rd Marines were stationed at Camp Schwab, which was in the northern part of the island of Okinawa. It was one of the newest bases and had very good training areas.

It was about this time that they started issuing the new rifle, the M14. This weapon was made by Springfield, and it had a 20 round magazine, whereas the M1 had an 8-round clip. Most people do not know it, but the manual of arms had to be changed also.

In the Marine Corps during my 20 years they issued three main weapons. The M1 came out during the Second World War and went through the Korean War. The M14 came out in the early 60s, and it was replaced with the M16 during my second tour in Vietnam in 1968. Each time the round (bullet) got smaller.

During the Korean War your rifle, BAR (Browning Auto Rifle) and machine gun all used the .30-caliber round. This ammo had great penetration, and the armor piercing would go clear through a telephone pole at 180 yards. The muzzle velocity was 2600 to 2800 per second, and the ammo came in three types. There were ball, tracer and armor piercing rounds. There was also blank ammo for training. The M14 used the 7.62, which is the NATO round. (A note of interest: the Navy Seals just brought the M14 back for special use.) One of the drawbacks for the M1 was the eight-round clips. If the rounds were not all in line, then the clip could not be pressed home in the receiver. When the last round had been fired, there was a loud ping that told everyone (including the enemy) the weapon was empty. All in all, I still loved this weapon.

Three weapons I left out are the carbine, the grease gun, and the 45 pistol. They were carried by crew-served weapons personnel. The carbine was too light with not enough knockdown power. The grease gun was carried by the pathfinder personnel; it had fixed sights and was only good at very close range.

Picture 19 – Pathfinders

I remember that with the weapon I had you could not hit a bull in the ass at five feet. On the range at 25 yards, I had to aim about six feet above the target and six feet to the right just to hit the whole target. The 45 pistol was carried by the command personnel, and I was carrying this weapon as a platoon sergeant. This was also used by crew-served personnel. Notice the grease gun on the first man, which was easy to carry while jumping.

The M16 used the 2.23 round, and when this weapon first came out there were a lot of problems. The muzzle velocity was 3200 feet per second, and with such a small round, the least object would send the projector spinning. It had been known to tear off a man's arm. The big problem with this weapon was that it jammed in the early days of the war. The chemicals that made up the powder of the projectile would build up (leaving a residue), and hence there would be clogging of the round in the chamber.

This cost a lot of people their lives during combat. Eventually the problem was corrected, and in the Gulf War the weapon did a great job. There are other devices that can be used on this weapon like a grenade launcher. It can also have a scope.

We returned to Camp Pendleton and became 1st Battalion 1st Marine Division. We were at the far northern end of the base. An order came out looking for instructors for a new school teaching guerrilla warfare. I liked the idea and soon was teaching at the new school. The officer in charge was Capt. Rice. He was to become a general later in his career. We had a free hand on making up our own training aids and lectures. We would give the other instructors our lectures and take advice on what worked and what did not. By the time we had made up a complete plan, we had a rifle company ready for a two-week course: one week of classroom and one week in the field.

The training was in the Cleveland National Forrest adjacent to Camp Pendleton. This was a very rugged area, which would have made an excellent training ground for guerrilla warfare. I wish the school had lasted longer, for it was the best course I ever had the pleasure to teach.

We were TAD (temporary additional duties), so when the Cuban missile crisis started, we were all ordered back to our outfit.

This action was so fast that we were taken to San Diego and loaded aboard the ship on the same day, each Marine given an armor vest. We were underway so fast that not all Marines had a bunk. During the first several hours they welded bunks over the hatch covers, and this had to do until we reached the Panama Canal. They then took off a company of Marines and loaded them aboard another ship.

There is probably not another outfit in the whole world that could have moved out as fast as the U.S. Marine Corps, to then be ready to fight upon arrival. We stopped at an island close to Cuba and had a practice landing.

With the new body armor the troops were so loaded down that we had a few causalities on the wet net training. They had made the new weapon (M 14) so the load would be lighter but with the combination of everything it had added so much more weight that if we had made a landing, a lot of troops would have been killed or wounded. The heat was just one of many problems. I learned years later that the Russians were thinking of using the A bomb if we had made the landing. Not landing there was the luck of the gods.

It was just before Christmas when we landed at Camp Del Mar boat basin. My new assignment was at the NCO (non commission officer) school. The school was at main side, and I was to teach NBC Warfare (nuclear, biological and chemical). I was teaching this course when we learned that President Kennedy was shot and later died (1963).

I had met my future wife, Denise, before we went on the trip to Cuba. She had written every day while I was gone. She was a nurse at Compton General Hospital, and a friend had told me about her. I had a trailer at Beach Lake Trailer Park, and when I returned she quit her job and moved in with me. Living here I had some of the happiest days of my life. She told me one day she was pregnant, so we got married. Our son Patrick was born and had red hair that stood out so much that everyone wanted to see what the father looked like. There was a picture on the wall of a redheaded baby, and I stole it. I meant to take it back, but the old hospital was torn down, and it did not belong in the new one.

Beach Lake was shutting down, and we moved to a small apartment near the Oceanside Pier. It was now 1965, and I had gotten orders to go to Hawaii with dependents. We were all excited and making plans when the Vietnam War started. The first thing they did was cancel the dependents. Denise was pregnant, and I had to find a place for her to stay. Her sister lived in Orange and wanted her to come up there. This was great, and we rented an apartment close to her sister. This was a big relief, for she had someone to keep her company while I was overseas. I flew to my new outfit in Hawaii which was 3rd Battalion 4th Marines 3rd Marine Division.

When I landed in Hawaii I learned that my outfit had moved out to Vietnam, and I was given a choice of staying or going on to Vietnam. Because I did not have my family with me, I chose to go.

I was loaded aboard a C-130 aircraft and took off for Okinawa. We spent a couple of days there getting shots and assignments and then flew to Da Nang, Vietnam. They then took me by helicopter to Phu Bai.

Chapter Ten

Vietnam

When my outfit arrived in Vietnam they were taken up the Perfume River to the city of Hue. They debarked and were moved to Phu Bai. Phu Bai had an Army commutation post there and a very large airfield. It was Easter Sunday when they arrived.

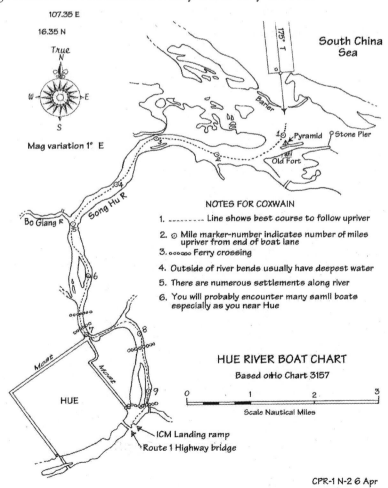

Picture 20 – Hue, Vietnam

The city of Hue would be destroyed during the Tet Offensive later in the war. At the present time we were allowed liberty there during the day. We had to take precaution while en route from Phu Bai to Hue because there were Viet Cong in the area.

While aboard the truck everyone had to face outward in case they threw a grenade in the truck. We would stop at an Army compound and turn in our weapons while on liberty. We had to be back in time for sundown. We had already set up a defense around Phu Bai. The foliage was very light in the surrounding area.

In the early days we spent most of our time stringing barbwire around the defensive of the base and patrolling both inside and up to the jungle outside the area. During the day we used the tents for resting and normal things like letter writing, cleaning weapons, etc. We would hold mail call and weapons inspection. As dusk fell we moved into our foxholes.

After a couple of months we started getting free mail service. For the record, it started in September 1965. All you had to do was to write "free" where the stamp normally goes.

To make it as easy as possible, we had four men in each defensive position. If there was trouble, we would go on either 50 or 100 percent watch. This, in the meantime, gave each man the most rest time possible

As time went on the action got hotter and hotter. In the beginning we had a few booby traps and signs that the enemy was around. We made longer patrols and even went into the rainforest looking for the VC. I loved the rainforest because it was cool, and things that you paid a lot of money for back home were there for the taking. You would not find anywhere in the world more beautiful orchids than they have there, growing wild.

There was what they called a triple canopy jungle. Some of the roots were exposed, and it was almost impossible to climb over them because they were higher than one could reach. We soon moved our outpost next to the rainforest. We selected a hill about 225 feet in elevation and started building bunkers for defense. There was a small river running along the rainforest to our front.

On the map this hill was called N Mo Cau (new MO COW). To help pass the time, we made up a song that had the tune from Roger Miller's "King of the Road." We named our song, "King of the Grunts." In my last book I put in this poem.

About this time my enlistment was up, and I raised my right hand for the last time. It was for the last four years of my 20-year enlistment. The date was August 5,1965. I did not realize that I would have to come back one more time.

Picture 21 – Lt. Kemper and Author

Picture 22 – Lt. Kemper Wounded

Lt. Kemper was my platoon leader, and it was near our outpost that he was badly wounded when he stepped on a land mine. We did not think he would live, but they got him to the aid station and he made it. We visited him once before they took him to the hospital in Da Nang. I always wondered what happened to him, but like so many others, he is gone with the wind. The other picture is me with the lieutenant. Notice only one dry spot on my uniform. This should tell why I'll never come back after the war is over. There were a lot that did come back, so I wrote the poem explaining my reason.

Picture 23 – The Only Shade for Miles

Memories of Phu Bai
Phu Bai, Phu Bai, the land of the Vietnamese,
Memories remain like long shadows of distant trees.
The sounds, the smells, the heat of that out of focus place,
Now the days come back like a faceless face.
We came and stayed, way too long, I think,
Wake up tomorrow, wishing and praying for a cold, cold drink,
The waste of it all, do not wake me from a timeless sleep,
For time waits not, for a bitter harvest to reap.
Blistering sun goes down on the land of the Vietnamese,
So still, so hot, Oh, God, what I'd give for a cool, cool breeze,
Like shadows in black, they came shifting and went,
Barbwire in place, we watched, waited, without content.

Some to this day go back to the land of the Vietnamese,
Not me, I still see the shadows of those distant trees,
Phu Bai, Phu Bai, I came, I saw, then drifted away.
Never to return, not now, not tomorrow, nor any other day!!!

We got orders to go to Da Nang. Our assignment was Perfume River. I would be coming back to this place on my next tour of duty. The hill was in a critical area. This was why the French built concrete bunkers during their time there. When they left they destroyed them. There was enough left that we could use them with a little cover overhead to keep out the rain.

The monsoon was now in full force. We had not been issued jungle boots, and we were still in the green utilities. The leather boots stayed wet all the time, and soon the troops started getting trench foot. We did not get the jungle boots until my second tour along with the camouflage uniforms. Our green uniforms were also coming apart.

There was an incident where we had a Marine up for court martial. Gen. Walt was paying us a visit at this time. As the general walked around the area, a young Marine was sitting and did not get up as the general passed by him. The general turned to the sergeant major and said, "I want this company commander relieved; the morale is too low."

Lt. Gen. Kulack also paid a visit to the hill. This should tell the reader how important this hill was. Gen. Kulack was the one who recommended Gen. Murray to take over the 5th Marines during the Korean War. Gen. Murray was a colonel, and there were many who were senior to him. He got the job, and the rest is history. There is a bridge named after Gen. Murray, and once more Gen. Kulack was there for the dedication.

The pleasure of your company is requested
at the dedication of the
Murray Bridge

In honor of
Major General Raymond L. Murray
USMC (Ret)

Thursday, 30 January 2003
9:00 o'clock in the morning
at the Bridge located at the
Intersection of North River Road
and College Boulevard
Oceanside, California

Regrets Only: Attire:
Call 760-757-4323   Civilian - Informal
                           Military - Uniform
                                of the Day

Picture 24 – Murray Bridge Dedication

My twins were born on September 21. We had moved off of Perfume River and were now guarding a railroad bridge. This was probably the most important bridge in Vietnam. In fact, I would guard this bridge on my second tour of duty. This is one bridge that the enemy never blew up.

The Dodgers won the World Series that year. I think this was one of the best teams the Dodgers ever had. Pitching for them that year was Sandy Koufax, Don Drysdale, Johnny Padres and relief pitcher, Ron Perranoski. I got to hear the game when Sandy Koufax pitched a no-hitter.

We went back to Phu Bai, and right away we had a hot assignment. An intelligence report showed a trail where the Viet Cong were bringing in supplies. We moved into the area, and my platoon got the assignment to set up across the trail. The rest of the company set up on our right.

We had so much fire support that I felt we were there only for the show. There was on station, naval gunfire, 105 mm and 155 mm artillery and mortars. It was around midnight when we heard them coming up the hill. We held our fire until they were close, and then we opened up. As we fired, all the supporting fire started putting up illumination, which made the area look like it was daylight.

You would have thought nobody could have lived through this. Yet when we checked out the impact area we found nothing. We spread out and started checking the surrounding area. With me there were three Marines, and we broke to the left and went along a creek bed with heavy foliage. A VC stood up and aimed his weapon, but we only heard a metal click before we killed him.

I reached down and picked up his weapon, a French submachine gun. My weapon at this time was the 45 pistol that I returned to the holster. We went a little further down the creek before we crossed over to the other side. We then started searching the bank back to where we started.

I saw a movement and lobbed a grenade. Sometimes things happen and one cannot explain. I saw to my surprise the grenade coming back, and it exploded, wounding me in the back. I felt my left arm go limp. I drew my pistol with my right hand and killed him.

As I returned to our CP (command post), there were several wounded enemies, one real bad, a couple of dead and eight others. These were the ones that were caught in the original ambush and rounded up in the search of the surrounding area. I relieved the two Marines so they could go back to their unit. At this time the search was still going on.

There were two South Vietnamese officers who had come along on this operation and later put us up for the Vietnam Cross of Gallantry.

As I guarded the prisoners, there were illuminations (rounds being fired). As the shells exploded, a parachute with a flare attached would float down while the steel container would drop with a screaming noise. It had the prisoners jumping around like herd of cattle about to stampede. I must admit that I was a little shook myself. I kept yelling and pointing that French submachine gun to keep control of them.

That one enemy who was badly wounded was crawling around with his guts dragging behind him, screaming in pain. When the corpsman returned I asked him to give the poor guy a shot to shut him up. The corpsman told me he could not do it because the morphine was for our troops only. I told him to either give the poor SOB a shot or kill him. He gave him a shot. The guy died shortly afterwards.

At first light a chopper came in to take the prisoners and me out. As I checked that weapon I found out why we were not killed when we first met the enemy. The magazine spring was broken. As the guy released the bolt and squeezed the trigger, the bolt did not pick up a round; hence forth, no round was fired.

My outfit was shipped back to Okinawa for refitting and replacements. I elected to stay in Vietnam to complete my tour of duty. Later I regretted this decision because Christmas came up, and not knowing anyone, it was one of the loneliest times of my life. I'll never forget when I heard Mahalia Jackson sing, "Oh, Holy Night," how I broke down and cried.

My new job was taking care of the POW compound. The outfit was going on sweeping action and would round up everything that might be the Viet Cong. Sometimes we had whole families in the compound. My time was up, and there was nobody there to say goodbye to. I could see how much Phu Bai had expanded and knew that it was just a matter of time before heavy battles would be fought here.

Chapter Eleven

Home & War

Exactly 13 months to the day I returned home. Denise was living in a house in Orange. It was good to see my family again. We went house hunting in Oceanside, and although I wanted to live in Carlsbad, I could not afford the price for a down payment. We bought a home on Foussat Road with a very large backyard and got a loan from Cal Vet, who was better than the VA. I'm still living in the same house after over 40 years and have 50 fruit trees and a good-size garden.

My mother-in-law, Mimi, came to live with us. She was one of the most interesting people I have ever known. She started the garden, and every now and then, she would want to make the garden bigger. I could only say yes.

My new duties were with ITR (Infantry Training Regiment). I was teaching both weapons and tactics. It was not too long before my recon background caught up with me. I was transferred to a recon school at Camp Horno. This was OK except there was one week of school and one week in the field, which meant I had less time with my family.

The time went by so fast that, before I knew it, I had gotten orders to go back to Vietnam. The two years had been good ones, and watching my kids grow up made it hard to leave them again. Those two Christmases together were a great joy, and I have never forgotten after all these years that they were among the best we ever had.

We had to go through training and were issued the new M16 rifle, which had just come out. On May 5, 1958, I departed El Toro for my second tour in Vietnam. El Toro is no longer a Marine Corps air station. It was closed down, and the Marines were moved to their new base in San Diego.

One good thing about this last trip was that we were flown by civilian airline, Continental Airlines, our new transportation. My first trip was by ship. My second trip was by military aircraft, and now we were coming up in the world. The stewardesses' names were Nancy, Rita, Christy and Trixie. They were very good to us Marines.

When we landed and they opened the door, that hot air hit me like a firestorm. It had all come back like a bad dream: Oh, my God, please help me—how am I going to take another 13 months? One of the stewardesses standing in front of me made me do a crazy thing. I took her in my arms like it would be the last thing I would do on this earth and kissed her. I always remember that she was wearing a soft pair of white gloves, and she kissed me back.

We were to spend a week getting acclimatized. They gave us something new: freeze dried steaks. All you did was open the can and add water. It was better than fresh steak. One thing I did not forget was those big black flies. Just as soon as the water was added they came out of nowhere and covered everything.

After a week they loaded us aboard a LCU (landing craft utility), and we were heading for the DMZ (Demilitarized Zone). They transferred us to a LST (landing ship tank). We rode all night and met up with an aircraft carrier called the USS Valley Forge.

We moved north, and after a night we loaded onto helicopters and were flown to Camp Carol. I could see a lot of people as we landed, and all of a sudden there was a loud explosion and everyone started running. It did not take a genius to figure out what had happened. There were incoming rockets, and I did like everyone else—I started running and hit the deck.

My new outfit was H Company 3rd Battalion 3rd Regiment 3rd Marine Division. I was now a platoon sergeant of the 3rd Platoon. It's funny when you think about it, but I had served in all three regiments and in all three battalions of the 5th, 4th and the 1st, and, would you believe, I was wounded in all three units.

Our first job was to guard a bridge that had been destroyed during the battle of Khe Sanh. It was near a river, which made it easy to get our water. The platoon had taken a lot of casualties before I arrived and was now down to below half strength. My platoon commander was a mustang (a commissioned officer who began his career as an enlisted service member).

Giant copter of the 1st Air Cav. Div.'s 470th Flying Crane Co. lowers
a prefabricated bridge into place along Highway 9. Army and Marine
engineers quickly reconstructed bridges that had been destroyed.
(USA Photo by SP5 John Pettway)

Picture 25 – Bridge in Khe Sanh, Vietnam

A few days after I joined the outfit we were sent on patrol. Leaving the river it was almost a straight climb uphill. It was a triple canopy jungle, but its advantage was that it was cool. Somehow we were able to penetrate a very large enemy camp. There were supply bunkers, hospital and many other bunkers for defense. The enemy had white markings for movement at night. I had a very weird feeling and told the lieutenant that we may be in deep trouble.

We needed water and sent a small unit to fill up the canteens from a stream up ahead. They were hit by automatic weapons as they filled up the canteens. Five were wounded, and with only 16 to start with, we had a problem and had to evacuate. Three of wounded were on the plane with me when we left the states.

We lucked out because three would be walking wounded. We put two on the point (at the front of the column) this included the lieutenant. Four would carry the wounded with two to relieve them. There were two with me as rear guard. We had artillery in support, but they could not get on target. The mortars also sent up fire support, but we could not locate where they were landing. I really do not know why the enemy did not attack.

About halfway back we came upon an area where there had been a bombing, and there was a clear area through the triple canopy jungle. We called for a Medevac. Soon there was a chopper on station. They had what is called a donut that could be lowered through the hole in the jungle. The first wounded was lifted with no trouble. The second one had a head wound, and about halfway up, the cable jammed. He was swinging blindly, and all of a sudden his pants fell off, leaving him naked. It was a very sad sight. He was lucky the helicopter could ease him through the clearing and lower him back down among friendly troops.

I was lucky myself to have made it. If it had not been able to cool off in the stream I would not have made it. I kept cramping up due to not being climatized to the heat of Viet Nam and was falling further and further behind. By the time I got there, I was shaking so badly (from shock) that they had to wrap me in a poncho. After a night of sleep I felt well in the morning.

Our next mission was to take Hill 512 during the battle of Khe Sanh. This hill had been taken but had been abandoned after the siege had lifted, and the enemy had reoccupied it. The Second Platoon got the job of taking it once more.

An air strike was called in, and soon the F4U Phantom was tearing the hill apart. The Second Platoon went in for the attack, but just at the base of the hill we heard a loud explosion and knew something bad had happened. The radio started calling for a Medevac. There had been 22 Marines in the Second Platoon, and now they had been hit with a claymore mine, wiping out over half of their number.

As they started evacuating the wounded, the call came over the radio for the Third Platoon to take over the attack. We passed through the Second Platoon and right in front of us was a bunker where the enemy had started the ambush. I ran to the left of the bunker and threw a grenade and stepped to the left again. It was a good thing I did because the bunker had a false front, and the explosive came right through, which could have killed me.

I did not mention that the Third Platoon had only 12 men. I kept it to myself that this was insane, but we had our orders, and we started up the hill. As we got to the top, the hill was broad at the right side where we stood. The lieutenant took half of the men to set up a base of fire, and I took what was left and started the attack.

We had only two M16s that would fire. The company had lifted their base of fire, so right away we killed two NVA (North Vietnamese Army). Those son-of-a-bitches had brand new AK-47s. We moved up their trench line using their own weapons. It was here that a sniper had me in his sights when one of my troops took him out. (Schmolke was his name, and he was killed later at An Hoa.)

I picked up the sniper's rifle and put my pistol back in the holster. The hill was very steep to our left. There was a bunker on the far side of the hill, and as we got close, the enemy started throwing grenades. Because the hill was steep, the grenades would roll by and explode down below. I kept yelling at that guy and calling him every nasty name I could think of. In the meantime I sent one of the Marines around behind his bunker with a LAW (anti-tank weapon), and when the Marine fired, it blew the NVA right out the front, killing him.

The company kept calling and asking if the hill was secure. I said, "Yes, but if the enemy does a counterattack, we do not have much to stop them." It was not too long before the company was there. We set up a 360 degree defensive around the hill. I was completely drained and fell to sleep right away. My platoon leader told me that he was putting me in for a medal. I never got anything. He was wounded a day later and I never saw him again.

The worst was yet to come. Early the next morning we started taking shell fire. The company moved back off the hill, leaving my platoon to hold on. We soon took three more wounded. One of the wounded was our corpsman. There were nine men left, which was not even a decent squad. We were in luck though because the enemy made very strong bunkers. I was by myself, and I could see the mortar shells landing. If you have never been under an attack like this, I can tell you that it is sheer terror. It seems like it goes on forever.

The next day we observed two NVAs just below us. They were wearing pit helmets kind of like the Marines wore during WW11 on the rifle range. They saw us and fired a rocket-propelled grenade, which wounded my platoon leader. He would be flown out soon, leaving me in charge now with seven men. The company returned, and we got orders to sweep around the hill. After leaving the hill the vegetation got very heavy until we reached a ridgeline just a short ways from our starting point.

Just as we moved along the ridgeline we heard mortars start to fire. There is a short time from the time you hear the plop of the shell leaving the tube until they land. It was this time we took off on the run, and as we looked back you could see where we had been covered with exploding shells.

Where we now stood the enemy had a line of bunkers which opened up, and we were in trouble once more. The bunkers were so well hidden that it took us a while to locate them. They lay just below where we stood. One of my Marines was behind a tree when the NVA opened up with a machine gun. One round went through the tree and hit his weapon, going through his magazine, smashing all the rounds and stopping just below the bolt of his weapon. This saved him but really screwed up his weapon.

We destroyed the enemy and passed on through. There came a distress call from a recon unit, but they were too far away, and soon the calling stopped. I never learned what happened to them, but I think they were wiped out. Now our company was so under strength that they pulled us out and sent us south to reorganize.

We picked up new men, and the third picked up a new officer. His name was Gibbs. Over a period of time I found him to be a fine officer. We were sent to Hill 190 not far from Da Nang. There was a river running just below the north side, and over a period of time the enemy had knocked out a couple of Amtrak (Amphibious Tractor) which had now rusted. I wrote a poem that was published in my last book about this scene. So out of place was a Vietnamese farmer still tilting the soil around this destroyed equipment.

Just before we left the hill we watched an Amtrak coming down the river. You could tell that there was an area on the river bank that had been used by the Amtrak before. The enemy knew this also and had mined the place. We watched as the Amtrak exploded and the troops inside ran out only to die. They were on fire and did not get too far before they died.

There was one more thing that happened before we left the hill. The Starlight Scope had just come out, and we got one for testing. We were in an ambush site and were told that a friendly patrol would pass through our area. I saw them all right. They were right in front of us. The scope did work but not well enough.

This had been good duty on Hill 190, and our next job was at a place called Thuong Duc. Usually one has a feeling about a place, and I had a bad feeling about this one. The camp lay between two rivers that came together at the base, forming a Y.

At first our company was across the river in a peanut field. We had the job of clearing any mines that the enemy lay on the road that went back to Perfume River. I hope the reader remembers that hill, for it was here that I spent some time on my first tour.

We would sweep about halfway and meet with a company coming from Perfume River. One of these companies had someone the whole country knew. That was Capt. Robb who had married President Lyndon Johnson daughter.

Every now and then we would lose a Marine. One day a tank ran over a mine, and the track blew up and hit a Marine, coming down in his chest, killing him.

The company was moving back but leaving my platoon. We were to join the camp across the river. Thuong Duc was run by the Green Berets along with irregular troops. They were a mixture of Chinese and Vietnamese. One day one of the Green Berets came over and told me that if they got overrun he would be coming to our lines.

I got the feeling this was not too good an outfit. The hill was divided into two parts. We had the left side to defend, and the Green Berets had the right side. We sent out patrols daily, and the signs showed us that there was a very strong enemy unit nearby.

We lucked out because we were pulled off the hill before the big attack. Just before we left we held a police call and stacked all our trash. There were always rations left that the troops did not eat, and the irregular forces went through the trash making a big mess looking for food.

The CO of the 5th Marines flew over the area and sent our CO a message that we had left a big mess. We had to send a squad back to hold another police call. As the chopper set down on the helipad, the enemy opened up with a recoilless rifle, killing most of the squad. The helicopter was able to lift off, but the rear of the chopper was open and dumped the corpsman out. He lived but lost both legs. Lt. Gibbs was relieved.

It was a very short time before the Stars and Stripes paper ran the story about thousands of the enemy overrunning Thuong Duc. This was one of those events I'll always have a bad feeling about: the waste of all those Marines. It was a stupid police call. I wrote a poem about this in my last book.

Chapter Twelve

Ambush and Patrol

The patrolling and ambush were constant. There was patrolling during the day, and the ambush party usually went out just before sunset and set in just before darkness. We were now located at the tank park just outside of Da Nang. We were able to get rest during the day and move out into the village just before sunset. We moved some of the Marines into ambush positions in areas where we thought the enemy would be moving.

Sometimes it worked, and then there were times when nothing happened. There was one classic example when it did work. Below is a special report of a squad-size ambush conducted on October 27, 1965

The Third Battalion S-3 reported that two bodies had been found at ambush site. The regimental intelligence officer and intelligence chief departed the regimental CP to given location of the bodies, weapons, equipment, etc. that might be made available.

The two bodies had been moved approximately 100 yards by the Marines to a point at the roadside of National Highway #1. The bodies were those of two male Vietnamese, estimated age was 25-30 years, both wearing short black pants, black shirts and coolie hats. Neither was wearing shoes. Death was due to multiple gunshots and fragmentation wounds. Each was carrying GVN and Viet Cong identification cards. Photographs of a GVN policeman who had been assassinated about one and one half weeks ago were found on their bodies.

The cartridge cases were found at several points where the Viet Cong had emerged prior to receiving the Marines' fire. A few cartridge cases were found at the dike where the Viet Cong delivered covering fire.

The ambush consisted of 12 men: 11 Marines and 1 corpsman. The unit arrived just before dusk. As the Marines arrived they heard the striking of wood, which they thought was a warning to the Viet Cong. They saw a flashlight believed to be a signal also.

At 2200 hours, the Marines became aware of movement along the trail to the west. The squad leader had already instructed the members to hold their fire until the last minute to allow the enemy to get to point blank range. The firing would be initiated by the M60 machine gun.

The machine gun was deep in the ambush area, and the forward Marines were 15 yards forward. The Marines were able to identify the intruders as the Viet Cong. Seven of the enemy had passed the position of the most forward Marine when they opened fire.

When the point Viet Cong reached the minimum range of the machine gun, the engagement was initiated by a steady, long burst of the machine gun, which was immediately accompanied by the combined weapons of the other members of the squad. The total of the time of the firing was about 60 seconds. All seven of the enemy who had entered the ambush had been killed. One of the Marines had been wounded. He was the one who originally observed the first movement. He had tossed two grenades at the hut, killing one Viet Cong.

The Viet Cong recoiling from the Marines' fire marshaled their forces and made a costly but adequate withdrawal. The Marine squad leader decided that a withdrawal was in order for his forces as well as the volume of the Viet Cong fire, the absence of panic and the movement and noise well to the rear and now to the flanks of a known Viet Cong element indicated that he was numerically outmatched

He first checked the Viet Cong casualties to ensure that they were dead. He checked the number of the bodies firing and in several cases bayoneted those who were not dead. The count was 15. Under the cover of grenades, M79, and small arms, the squad withdrew from the ambush position in an orderly but hasty movement. They redeployed to the east of National Highway #1 in a position approximately 150 meters north of the last position. They were now receiving heavy fire, so they requested 81mm mortar fire support. They already had one casualty.

At this time they started receiving heavy fire, causing their second casualty. The 81mm mortar open firing adjusted fired the second round and then fired for effect. The squad leader directed the fire back to the ambush site. A total of 60 rounds were fired when the squad leader terminated the mission. The Viet Cong fire had ceased, and the squad's opposition had disappeared. The squad was able to continue its withdrawal to the company CP without incident.

The engagement had not yet run its course. The Viet Cong had withdrawn along its route of arrival. The indications were that the Viet Cong, burdened with casualties, would be forced to proceed slowly back to a close by hamlet. On this logical and probable location, a total of sixty 105mm rounds were fired. Additional artillery and mortar fires were scheduled to isolate this area, increasing the hazards to the Viet Cong if they attempted to displace to a different location.

The chronology of this engagement is of particular importance. The Marines were in position less than 15 minutes before the action was initiated. Upon the arrival of the Marines, the villagers in the area commenced to sound what were likely warning signals. The appearance of lights on the east side of the highway indicated that a small scout party may have cleared the area of the ambush site prior to the arrival of the Marines, only to have Marines occupy the position just in time to intercept the larger unit.

The reaction of the Viet Cong, although disciplined and professional, suggested that the ambush found them unprepared and temporarily confused. The short duration of the firefight and the rapid commencement of mortar fire provided little opportunity for the Viet Cong to accurately assess the opposition. Their subsequent actions were in agreement with these assessments.

Just before we left the tank park a strange thing happened at the staff club. We were sitting around when one of the staff sergeants of the tanks walked in and started firing his 45 pistol. I have never seen a club clear out so fast. I do not know what made me do what I did next, as I had neither run nor ducked. I walked up to the guy firing his weapon and held out my hand for the gun. He had a strange look on his face like someone in another world. He handed me the weapon and collapsed on the floor. I stood there until the MPs came. I felt that, after going out every night putting my life on the line, I was not up to this shit. I never learned what happened to him.

I was now the company gunnery sergeant. We had also gotten a new company commanding officer. His name was Moore. He turned out to be a fine CO, and I wished we would have had him before many of the past events had happened.

Our new job was protecting that railroad bridge that I had guarded on my first tour. Our company was spread out on both sides of the river, but luck was once more with us. We had a small boat that made my job so much more pleasant.

The platoons had to get their rations, ammo and mail, so I would go out at least once a day for a boat ride to deliver the goods. If I wanted a little fresh fish for dinner, all I had to do was drop a grenade in the river and wait a minute and fish would float to the top. The picture on the front of the book of me was taken at the bridge.

To protect the bridge from enemy frogmen we would drop blocks of TNT in the river from time to time just in case they had any funny ideas. The time would vary so they could not time the event. My wife had just sent me a ring with my birthday stone in it. It was just a little too big for me. As I threw a block of explosive in the river, my ring went along for the ride. I have never owned another ring since.

I have a good friend who served with me in Stormy Sexton's outfit. He was now so far back in the rear that when I invited him to come to the bridge and take a boat ride, he had to decline because he was in a top secret position. Louis Shore was his name, and he retired down in gaitor bait territory. We had been staff sergeants in 3-3, but Louis got a commission after attending language school. We still keep in touch.

Nothing lasts forever, and we got new orders to go to a place called An Hoa. This would be a very unhappy place for our company. This area was the 5th Marines' responsibility, and we were now attached to them.

Just before we left the bridge I was starting to have a hard time seeing anything very clearly. After an exam the doctor told me I needed glasses. I made a comment, and the doctor said," Hell, Gunny, you are getting older." I was only 36, but in the Corps that is old.

Chapter Thirteen

From Tank Park to An Hoa

The company had 167 officers and men when we arrived at An Hoa. Two weeks later we were at the count of 72. This place was a real meat grinder. The other companies took a collection of 100 men and sent them to us. A short time later we were back to 67. It was due to booby traps, snipers, sickness and rotation.

We were flown in by helicopters, and our objective was to occupy a hill we had received no intelligence about. This hill was not too high, but it was now dark. The trouble had already started. First, I heard an explosion and the yelling of men now hurt, calling for a corpsman. Being the company gunny, I was at the very end of the column, so it took some time to learn what had happened. A short time later another explosion and three more men were hurt, one wounded real bad. He was carrying flares, and the explosive set them off, burning the Marine. I can hear him screaming even now.

There was a light mist, and as we covered the objection, we were still receiving harassing fire. We soon silenced it. I pulled my poncho over me and tried to get some sleep. The helicopters came in and took out our wounded.

The next morning we found the hill to be covered with mines and booby traps. It was a good thing we did not move around too much when we were receiving that harassing fire the night before. They moved the company back so we could destroy the obstacles.

We had a long rope with a hook on the end. I was involved because we did not have too many who could do this kind of work. After we discovered the booby trap or mine, we would put the hook on the trip wire and walk to the far end of the rope and pull. This usually exploded the booby trap. You would put a small explosive by the mine and blow it up, if it did not have a trip wire.

Most of the booby traps were either a can with a grenade in it or a can with a friction cap and an explosive charge. When one walked by and tripped off the booby trap, it would usually take off one leg, or if your feet were together it would take off both feet.

Even an old salt like me would screw up. We located a booby trap and put the hook on the trip wire, and as I walked to the length of the rope, I passed the place where we had slept the night before.

As I passed the sleeping bag where my old right guide had slept, I heard a pop, and I knew right away that it was a grenade. I took off running. The explosive caught up with me and knocked me off my feet. I had both arms out, and I took shrapnel in each one. It would have been worse if I had not been wearing my flak gear. His pack had taken most of the explosive and had been torn to shreds. This would be my third Purple Heart.

It is funny that when I received my third Purple Heart, I was in the hospital, and a Marine colonel came in to give me the award. He knew right away that someone had screwed up. His orderly had put two gold stars in the ribbon of the medal.

When one receives the Purple Heart, his first is with the medal. All others are a gold star in lieu of the medal. He now had to give me the medal. I often wondered after he got his orderly alone what he did to him

Picture 26 – Purple Heart

I also wondered how many people got two medals. Now I not only had flown the Stars and the Bars over U. S. property, but I had gotten an extra medal. I never wanted to become a problem, but here I was.

As the corpsman came over to check out my wound, the rain was coming down harder. He put pressure to stop the bleeding and put dressings on both arms. I was still in shock but getting real cold now. When I was put aboard the chopper, there were Marines with dogs and several prisoners aboard. The dogs were right on top of the enemy, and the fear was showing on their faces.

Sitting the chopper down at Da Nang, we were rushed into the hospital. All those wet clothes were taken off, and before I knew it, I awoke in the ward in a warm, dry bed. The wounds were not bad, and they had taken out many small fragments, many would come out on their own over time.

We had a USO Show while I was in the hospital. It was Gypsy Rose Lee. She came around and gave each patient a picture of herself. She has passed away now, but I will always have a soft spot in my heart for her. I remember during the Korean War how Debbie Reynolds sent all the guys in my outfit a picture of her. I still have that picture with a little Korean mud on it. I always wanted to return it and thank her for her kindness. Ten days after I was wounded, I returned to my outfit.

The company had taken a lot of casualties. We passed over an old rail track that now had only the gravel bed left. Upon examining the bunkers that the enemy had made, we could see where all the missing parts of the railroads were. They were so strong that even a B52 strike did not damage them too much. I wrote a poem about this event, and it was published in my last book. We stayed only a couple more weeks before we went to Liberty Bridge.

Picture 27 – Author

We were now at Liberty Bridge. This bridge had been blown up several times. There was a station near the bridge. I had a unit of Seabees make me an ashtray out of a 105 shell. They cut the shell about five inches from the base. I had a .50 caliber shell that had been fired by a F4U aircraft. They put it on the medal tube that was on the base of the shell. They then cut two 7.62 empty shell cases in two and brazed them to the outer rim of the 105 shell. These were used for resting the cigarette while smoking.

There was a 106 recoilless rifle there. On top of the recoilless rifle was a .50 caliber spotting rifle. You could hit a target a long way off with it. We saw the enemy crossing a rice paddy. They were so far away that you could not see them with the naked eye. Looking through the scope, the gunner would wait until they were halfway across and then fire. The round would hit the target and blow it apart. As quick as the sniper rifle was fired, the gunner would fire a beehive round which spread out and killed everything in its path.

Picture 28 – Goodbye, An Hoa

We got replacements, and those who had been here for a tour of duty were sent to the rear for shipment home. On the company roster I would put the new names marked the troops going home on rotation. I brought the roster back with me to the states. It told of those killed in action (KIA) and the date, those wounded in action (WIA), those who went on R&R, those who were in sickbay, those who had gone home. This roster was now in the hands of our reunion personnel.

I now had 10 months in the country, and they usually sent the staff NCO and the officers back to the rear after eight months. The sergeant major came out to the field, and I brought this to his attention. In less than a week I was sent to the battalion area for duty. My new assignment was taking over the enlisted club as manager. Would you believe that I was out of combat but got an increase in my pay?

Chapter Fourteen

Club and Home

When I went to the rear I took a couple of short timers with me. One had come over on the same airplane as me. His name was Jim Pomish, and he would join the Maricopa Sheriff Office. He is now retired after 26 years in Mesa, Arizona. Jim is on the left.

Picture 29 – The Enlisted Club

The club was not much. It had no security and had lost a lot of supplies and booze in the past. We borrowed a truck and went to the landing area where the ships docked. We now started scrounging lumber, cement, screen wire, nails, tools and any other thing that might be of use in building a real club.

Each day we could see the fruit of our labor. Soon we had a secure area to put in the supplies needed to run a club. We traded for an ice-making machine. One of the big problems was the termites. One day a whole swarm came out of the floor. We got some DDT and that solved the problem. We then put rock planters down the middle of the club and screen wire on all windows and doors. Then we got some beautiful plants, and the club was in business. The name of the new club was Hard Core Grunt.

If a person was a crook, there was a ton of money to be had. The troops had all kinds of kitty jars to get things like skin flicks and others things they wanted. We would find someone going on R&R and have them buy the flicks. I remember one of those films where there were two girls that brought down the British Government. It seemed like they had sex with the prime minister and with a Russian spy. Their names were Maundy Rice Davis and Kristen Keeler.

One day the chaplain came by the club, and that shut down the showing of skin flicks. We built a concrete rock entranceway with a big Marine CORPS emblem embedded in it.

There was a big operation outside of Da Nang. Many deserters were high jacking trucks and had built up a stronghold to collect the loot. Our company held a sweep and rounded up most of the deserters and all their supplies. There were several hundred cases of beer collected, and they gave half to my club. I could have sold that beer and kept the cash, for there was no way of knowing where it went.

Two things in leadership are; to accomplish the mission and to provide for the welfare of your troops. I made sure that our troops got all that beer for free. One thing happened that left a bad taste in my mouth. Our battalion was transferred to another camp, and the forward echelon came and took over the club for the officers because it was now the best club in the area.

Picture 30 – The Club

71

Picture 31 – Also At The club

The company was pulled from the field, and the first thing in order, was a ceremony for our dead from An Hoa. We placed a sandbag for each dead Marine, attached a bayonet to a rifle and stuck it into the sandbag. A helmet was placed on top of the rifle. Taps were played. Later I wrote a poem which has now become famous.

Picture 32 – Memorial Service

Ray: Thanks for bringing up the An Hoa Squad poem, Colonel Regal was right, Staff Sgt. Canada was the author, and I have attached it to this email. For those of us that were in An Hoa and at the memorial service, no one could have said it better; the words bring it all back just like the photo on the cover of our memorial flyer in Louisville.

Farewell to An Hoa Squad
Staff Sgt. James Jeep Canada
From his book, *We Few – We Chosin Few*

> Gone forever the An Hoa squad, what price glory
>   Known but to God,
> Each paid in full, farewell to arms, safe passage
>   Young warriors, away from harm;
>
> Long be green meadows, white be your cross,
>   Gallantly fought your battles, sadly be your loss,
> Taps played in honor, helmets placed side by side
>   Solemn shadows saluted, bidding goodbye;
>
> Those ten thus departed, this An Hoa Squad
>   Replaced by others where they once trod;
> Instilled with your memories, in a column of three,
>   Marched off together to pay their own fees;
>
> Gone forever when more battles are won, what
>   Price glory, among you my sons,
> Each pays to order for the bearing of arms,
>   Uptight tomorrow, in the way of harm.

March 3, 1969 in Memoriam For:
  LCpl. G.L. Thomas TX
  PFC R.A. Van Wombeke ILL
  LCpl. A.H. Terrell ARIZ
  PFC C I. Newberry KY
  LCpl. D.J. Turner MASS
  PFC J.M Schmolke La
  LCpl. D.P. Gallagher
  Cpl J.H. Porter
  HM-3 J.H. Durham OH
  Pvt J.J. Wiley NJ

Right after this happened there was one more thing that almost cost me my life. I had to pick up a truck and go to Da Nang for two pallets of beer. The driver was a young Mexican Marine whose wife had just had a baby. I had a map case with over $22,000 that belonged to the club.

There was a bridge about half way that the enemy had blown up. It now had a detour where you moved around the right side, and at the top you turned right and you were back on the highway. The driver, instead of turning right, went straight ahead into 60 feet of water upside down. I'll never forget how warm the water was.

My first impulse was to take off my flak jacket. I could not because the map case was over the flak jacket. I now thought I was going to die. I relaxed and took off the map case, then the flak jacket. I was able to crawl through the open window and floated to the top of the river. My young driver could not swim, so I grabbed him by the back of his jacket and dragged him into the shoreline. Now we were in Indian country without a weapon. We looked like two drowned rats. I saw the map case floating down the river, so I dove in and retrieved it. I would still be writing up a report on the club's money if I had not.

Soon a truck loaded with Seabees drove by and picked us up and gave us a ride back to our unit. I went in and got a new pistol, holster, a flak jacket and a new driver, I went to Da Nang and got two pallets of beer for the club. What a day—but it all ended well. We now moved to a new area.

The new area was a big mess, and their enlisted club was worse than the old one. Before I left the battalion, the officer and men gave me a plaque as a token of my hard work on the club. I had not only gotten extra money for running the club, but I was somewhat safe.

Picture 33 – Plaque

It is strange; you always remember how you went to war but cannot remember how you came home. I do remember how some of the people in San Francisco hated us service men. There was one hippie with long hair and dirty finger nails flipping me off and telling me to go fuck myself. Another female called me a baby killer. I almost lost my cool when one tried to spit on me. I wanted to get home so bad that I was afraid that I would be held up if I kicked their asses.

Chapter Fifteen

Discharged once more

The Marine Corps came up with a program called Projection Transition. It was for grunts like me. It was designed to teach you a trade before you got out of the service. It let you work for someone for 40 hours a week free while the employer taught you a trade. For any hours over 40 the employer paid you for the extra time. Most Marines never heard of this program.

You were to go back to the base once every two weeks to get paid. Then two weeks before you were discharged you had to come in for a medical checkup and all the discharge paperwork. Would you believe that I was stuck with duty on my last night in the Marine Corps?

In Project Transition I went to work for a cabinet maker named Ed Link. He was from Germany and really knew his trade. I enjoyed this job, and although I would end up going to welding school later, this knowledge helped me get a higher rating when I went to work for the Civil Service.

When you are discharged you go to the unemployment office to report that you are unemployed. They have veteran representatives who help you adjust to civilian life. The guy told me there was a wide open market for welders and that he could get me in school for the training that I needed for that job. He then told me I could collect unemployment while going to school and that my GI Bill would pay for the school. That was In addition to the retirement income that was half of my Marine Corps pay. I was making more than I did in the Corps.

I went to South Bay Trade School and took the unlimited welding course that taught arc welding, mig welding, brazing and helio—arc welding. I graduated first in my class. The school told me I could take ship fitting, and it would not be considered a change of a course. I was taking ship fitting and was building an outside shelter for the students' lunch area. I had an unlimited certification in welding and a certification for ship fitting.

While I was doing that job for the student lunch area, the foreman from Campbell Machine stopped by and watched me for a few minutes and told me that if I wanted a job to report to the shipyard the next morning.

I have written about this in my last book, so I'll only touch lightly on these events. I took the job and fell 80 feet and was hurt really bad. I eventually went back to work at the shipyard only to get hurt once more. Then I was laid off.

The state gave me a test that said I should be an accountant, so they sent me to school. The local college had already started, so I went to a business college. The next semester I enrolled at Mira Costa College. Before it was through I received an A.A. Degree in business.

I then enrolled in Pepperdine University and almost got my bachelor's degree before my GI Bill ran out. I needed five units to receive the degree, but I needed money also, so with three kids, I had to get a job.

I have to backtrack and talk about Agent Orange, which is now affecting my health. I was lying in that jungle along the DMZ when a C130 flew overhead. I could not see the plane, but soon I could smell the agent. The smell was just like something that one would put on their garden, and they dropped the chemical on us.

Of course, we got our water from a local stream, and it was contaminated. We did not think anything about it at that time. Soon all the leaves in that triple canopy jungle were falling. When this was all over it would affect millions of lives.

It would take a long time before our own government would except their responsibility and admit that it was their fault. In the meantime, I had come down with a problem with my prostrate and had to have an operation. I then came down with diabetes.

In the beginning, to receive a disability (I was receiving 10 percent), they would take 10 percent from your retirement, so you were not really receiving any increase in pay. It would take years before I got any money from the government.

It was by luck that I joined the Chosin Few origination in the year 2000. This was 31 years after I had retired. We had a meeting once a month and we would have special people to speak to us. One such person was Mike Schuman, who told us that if you had, say, a foot injury, you would eventually start having a problem with your knee and then hip and so forth. He also said that if you were receiving a disability, then he could get you more. I had put in for years on frostbite, Agent Orange, wounded three times and injuries from parachute jumping. Mike called the VA Hospital, and they confirmed they had my records on these claims. In no more than two months my disability claim jumped from 10 to 90 percent. First I received a check for back time, which was quite large; later, I received an upgrade to 100 percent and another check. The only trouble was that they took 100 percent from my retirement, which meant that I now received no retirement money at all.

It would take several years more before Congress passed a bill allowing those who retired and getting disability to receive both of their checks. The reason was that there were people getting disability who in some cases only had a few months in the service.

Now that we have not received a cost of living increase in three years, our standard of living is decreasing. However, our active military have received two pay increases in the last three years. A private is making more than I did when I retired as an E-6 with 20 years of service. It was only because of the cost of living that I could keep my head above water.

I do not think that we would mind taking a fall, but our Congress has increased their pay in the meantime. I am lucky that I get more than one government check, but those who have to make it on just a Social Security check are not keeping their heads above water.

A couple of years ago when the Osprey crashed, killing all aboard, a memorial service was held at the northern end of Camp Pendleton. The commandants of the Marine Corps, along with other high ranking officers, were in attendance. The service was held in a tent, and all those who were killed had their equipment laid out with the name of each Marine placed on it. The rain came down so hard that in all the years I have lived in California, I have never seen it rain this hard. Then the wind started, and on several occasions the tent was almost blown away. It was only because those young Marines were holding it down.

This was our outfit during the Korean War. The unit bought a beautiful arraignment of flowers. Eddie Flynn and I would represent H-3-5, and it was very sad. One father knelt beside his son's outfit and was crying uncontrollably. We all felt the pain in silence.

The aircraft has been corrected, and it is now ready to take the troops into battle or bring them back. There was a time that they almost scrapped it.

Over the years, I have attended the reunion for H-3-5. Although I did not start until 2000, I have watched the members slowly melt away. I attended the last one which was held in San Diego. It was sad to remember that in 2000 we took a picture of three Marines and a Navy corpsman in the same position of the four of us that was taken in Korea in 1951. In 2011, I was the only one standing. I do not think that I will be going to any more reunions.

I told the reader that I would tell about the scam that I was taken in on.

NORTH COUNTY TIMES
Feb 18 2011
Father swindled trying to help son
Retired Marine conned into wiring funds to "son" in Spain.

The phone rings and James Canada, a disabled 78-year-old retired Oceanside veteran, answers. It was his 46-year-old son, Patrick, and he was in trouble.

The story goes on to tell of my son winning a contest on the radio and going to Spain. In Barcelona he met a couple of guys who offered him a ride. The cops pulled them over and told them they were under arrest on drug charges.

My son let me talk to a person I thought was working for the embassy. He said that my son was in trouble and needed money for court expenses.

The voice sounded just like Patrick, and my wife thought it was him also. Patrick said, "Dad, do not say anything to anyone." I thought he was talking about his mother and wife, so I agreed. After three days and about $10,000, some things did not add up. Each time I called, the amount was the same, and Weston Union was the way they wanted the money sent.

I found out later that it did not matter what name or where you thought the money was going, because the person only needed the number on the wire sent to collect the money.

The last straw was when the phony told me that Patrick had misplaced his passport, and they needed the same amount. ($2700.00 was the max amount that you could send by

Western Union on each transaction.) I got mad and told them that I had no more money. They asked if there was anyone else that they could call. I said no.

The next day I called my son at his home. When he answered, I was so happy he was home safe. Only to find out he had never been anywhere. Then I told him about the scam. He did some checking and found out that the scam was not from Spain but in Canada

The real trick was when I thought Patrick asked me not to say anything to anyone. That made this scam work along with my past experience of being in jail in Mexico.

Chapter Sixteen

Reunion and E-mail

I had a friend who was holding a reunion for H-3-5 in San Diego in the year 2000. I helped him set up that reunion. His name was Easy Ed Flynn, and it turned out to be one of the largest numbers of members attending. The next year it was held in Oregon. When I returned I read in the local paper that the Chosin Few were to be the guests of honor for the 4th of July parade. I put my name in and joined the group. You would not believe it, but I was to ride behind my old regiment commander, now Gen. Murray. He is 88 years old but still looks good.

Picture 34 – Gen. Murray

He had joined the Chosin Few, and we would see him once a month at the El Camino Country Club. For the reunion in 2000, Ed and I paid the general a visit to invite him to be our guest of honor at the reunion. His wife answered the doorbell, and as she opened the door, there was a large picture facing you of Gen. MacArthur and then Col. Murray. On their living room wall were pictures of past presidents and one of Hubert Humphrey. I asked if Gen. Murray was a Democrat. She laughed and said, "Oh, my Lord, no!" The good general was out playing golf at the time, and we told her why we had come.

Two days later, she passed away, and we all knew why the general could not attend the reunion. Before he joined the Chosin Few dinner at the country club he would later, marry a lifelong friend who would also attend the meeting. I would help her when she wrote her book after he had passed away.

When I held my book signing at Barnes and Noble, there was a first sergeant and Gen. Murray, who would also have book signings. I gave my presentation first, and the first sergeant came up and said, "That's a tough act to follow." When he was through the general said, "That's two tough acts to follow." He was a very humble man who held three Navy Crosses.

Over time I have received email and would like to share a few with you. They came from people I have, in most cases, never met. The first one though is from Lou Buell, who was with me in Vietnam. I have a picture that we took together.

Picture 35 – Lou Buell and Author

I sent a message to all on the Marine Corps birthday, and I quote," Bless them all. On this day only a few can say, I was a Marine, so to you few I say with pride, HAPPY BIRTHDAY."

Lou responded with the following email:

"I was one of the few proud veterans to make it through the Chosin in Korea and Dodge City in Vietnam. You were an inspiration to us green combat Marines during my time in the field. I will never forget during the monsoon season when you put a rope on your ankle, a 45 in your mouth and swam across the current (not knowing what might be on the opposite side), then tied a rope so everyone else could hold on and wade across—straight out of a John Wayne movie."

P.S. What Lou forgot to mention was the leeches that covered us from head to foot when we got out of the water. The bug juice that each Marine carries would take care of this problem in a very quick way.

I saw the same kind of leadership in 2000 when James Jones, the commandant, went on the first Osprey flight after they were decommissioned for a year because of the crashes. My son at MCAS New River was also on board. I did not sleep much the night before, knowing he was going to be on it. The commandant led the way.

Semper Fi (we missed you at San Antonio) From Daniel W. Schmolke—Captain, Station 23 St. Tammany Parish Fire Protection District 23 Madisonville, L Louisiana

Thank you for your email. I read the poem this morning, and it brought a tear to my eye. The nickname runs in the family, as me and my dad both have it. Any more information you may have, like what unit/platoon he was with, any funny stories etc . . . would be appreciated. Thank you once again for the email and your service to this country!

My email:

I knew this fine young Marine, and up along the DMZ he saved my life. Smokey was his nickname, and a sniper had me in his sights when he shot the sniper dead. I picked up the sniper's rifle, which had great scope on it, and it was almost brand new.

This kid was real quiet, and I am very proud to have known him. He was killed not too long after this at a place called An Hoa. He was one of those I wrote the poem, "Farewell to the An Hoa Squad," about. If you would like a copy of this poem, I would be happy to send you one.

His follow-up email:

Thank you for the book information. It made me smile, knowing you wrote about my uncle in your book. I look forward to reading about the sniper rifle and your 20 years in the Corps. Thank you again, sir!

Jack Stubbs wrote the following e-mail:

Jeep,

Thank you for sharing your tribute poem. It is the first time I have seen it. It brings back both good and bad memories. Two of the Marines listed were friends of mine in the 1st platoon, Jim Porter and Dan Gallagher, who were killed by the same booby trap. Jim was my best friend, and the loss of his life was the biggest failure ever in mine. My son is named after Jim. Let me share a situation with Dan Gallagher. A few days before he was killed we were on night patrol, and I had lost my last pair of glasses after diving into a rice paddy. I was unable to see, and Dan held one end of a towel I had while I held the other end to guide me around until we finished the patrol. Dan was always looking out for his brother Marine.

They have never gotten old because every time I think about them or look at their pictures they are still young Marines.

Picture 36 – Vietnamese Money

Lou Buell wrote the following message

Rich

Got this picture from Jack Stubbs (*picture not included*). The picture was taken at the Cau Do Bridge. Crawley is on the left and Gallagher on the right. Crawley was WIA and Gallagher KIA in An Hoa on January 21, 1969. Just behind them is the lookout tower where you took a picture of me flexing my biceps (they had the 50 cal mounted in it).

From Lou Buell

About 5 years ago I was at IBM, Rochester, (I have been with IBM since1973), and at lunch I was walking through the mall, and I saw a deck, The Wall Shop, that had several pictures on easels displayed outside. From a distance I could see The Wall with someone holding an American flag against it. I thought even though 58,000 names are on the wall I would check for someone I knew, even though the odds were slim to none. Just to the left of the top of the flag there was "Gerald L. Thomas", Tex, I was stunned. The lady who ran the store came out and asked if I was OK. She said that it looked like I saw a ghost. I then explained to her the circumstances and bought a copy of the poster (Image Conscious #M632). I have attached a couple pictures of it—I have it on the wall in my recreation room.

Also attached are pictures I got from Texas classmates that they did for their 40-year high school reunion and one of his gravesite, plus a picture of him and Moriarty. Texas classmates and" Mo" have bought copies of the poster as well.

Picture 37 – Texas Classmates

Picture 38 – Gerald L. Thomas Grave Marker

Picture 39 – Vietnam Memorial Wall with Gerald L. Thomas Name Engraved

We missed you, Gerald!

Galena Park High School
Galena Park, Texas
Class Of 1964
40 Year Reunion   October 9, 2004

Picture 40 – Texas Reunion

From A Alvarez

Jeep received your book, thanks. I read it in two sittings. I thought it was great. I like to read about Marine history and of you. You are a living history. My neighbor wants to read it, so I am going to let him read it, and he must return it or I will blow his house up. His son is a Marine recruiter in Seattle, WA. I had not read a whole book in many years. I found your book unable to put down until I read it all. Thanks for the book and memories, especially the time in An Hoa when you were wounded with Kilo 3/1. I remember that night only because I was there with you. Semper Fi.

Taps for All

Taps always sad, many times our
Eyes do mist,
Life's long roll call, goodbye with a
Farewell kiss.
Marines all know so with their history
So instilled,
Always faithful my lads for its everlasting,
God's will.

Shoulders back, chest out now let me hear
Those heels.
Sound off, there the echo through the hills
As you lower the flag and play the slow
Lonesome taps,
Render that sharp hand salute for your time
Will come that is no perhaps.